TO

_____

FROM

_____

DATE

_____

BLESSED
ASSURANCE
JESUS IS MINE

OLD-TIME DEVOTIONS
FOR FRESH STARTS

DaySpring
LIVE YOUR FAITH

CONTENTS

BLESSED ASSURANCE

AND WE ALL, WHO WITH UNVEILED FACES
CONTEMPLATE THE LORD'S GLORY,
ARE BEING TRANSFORMED INTO HIS IMAGE
WITH EVER-INCREASING GLORY.
II CORINTHIANS 3:18 NIV

Blessed assurance, Jesus is mine!
Oh what a foretaste of glory divine!
Heir of salvation, purchase of God,
Born of His Spirit, washed in His blood.

This is my story, this is my song,
Praising my Savior all the day long;
This is my story, this is my song,
Praising my Savior all the day long.

As the beloved hymn reminds us, our lives are an ever-unfolding story of God's goodness and grace. They're filled with unique experiences, heartwarming connections, unexpected blessings, and yes . . . times of uncertainty too. The journey can be a marvelous one, but it won't be an easy one for any of us. We have lessons to learn and wisdom to gain, new things to discover about ourselves and our Maker, and old things to surrender that are no longer part of His plan for us. We are being remade in the image of Christ, and a lot goes into that! But when we walk closely with Jesus, we live with a sense of peace and assurance unlike anything we could experience without Him. And the times in our lives when that can be most evident are those times when we experience change. Exciting opportunities, big transitions, new perspectives, unexpected losses, first-time adventures, tough decisions, relationship and role shifts . . . and everything in between. What do all those things have in common for us? They can all be rich experiences that help to bring about our growth, healing, and wholeness, when we keep Christ at the center. They are opportunities to trust Him, to grow closer to Him in new ways, and to learn that our faith is far more than just words, and infinitely deeper than just hoping for the best. When we allow our spiritual muscles to be built in these times of uncertainty, we come out the other side with a deeper awareness of ourselves, greater compassion for our neighbor, and an even more authentic connection with our Maker. Because here's the truth: we can listen to all the wonderful messages in the world, but until we walk them out in our real lives, they remain just words. Change is a catalyst for our deeper reliance on God. It's one thing to *say* we believe in Him, place our hope in Him, and find peace in Him. But it's another thing to step out on that faith and discover that there truly is a solid foundation we have been given in Christ. There is a calm center within us, His Holy Spirit, that we can return to again and again for assurance and guidance through anything.

Loving Father, thank you for orchestrating it all
and bringing everything in my life together for our good
and Your glory. Remind me, Father, that my faith is
not wishful thinking, but a real connection with a real Creator.
While I live in ever-changing times, You never change,
and Your love and care for me never runs out.

AMEN

9

HE LEADETH ME

TRUST IN THE LORD WITH ALL YOUR HEART,
AND DO NOT LEAN ON YOUR OWN UNDERSTANDING.
IN ALL YOUR WAYS ACKNOWLEDGE HIM,
AND HE WILL MAKE STRAIGHT YOUR PATHS.
PROVERBS 3:5–6 ESV

Sometimes when God calls us to take hold of something new, He's asking us to let go of something else . . . and as most of us know, that's not necessarily an easy task. That *something*—or some*one*—may have been a very good gift. Maybe it was a connection or a commitment that gave us comfort in a difficult season of life or an anchor in a time of uncertainty or some healing right when we needed it. It's tough to imagine willingly letting go of what has served us well, but it may be just what we need in order to embrace the new thing He has for us. Perhaps it's another kind of connection He's asking us to release, one that He knows is *not* good for us—an addiction or a relationship that is dragging us down, hindering our health, or squelching our spirit . . . even when we can't see it happening.

If we're going to let Him lead us on this journey, it's best to allow Him to choose our companions—the people and the things He knows will bring about our greatest good and His glory. We can't know today what He'll ask us to leave behind tomorrow, but one thing we *can* always count on is this: *He will be with us, every step.* He'll always be preparing the way, leading the way, and making it possible for us to follow. Just as the hymn "He Leadeth Me" points out:

He leadeth me: O blessed thought!
O words with heavenly comfort fraught!
Whate'er I do, where'er I be,
Still 'tis God's hand that leadeth me.

And when "He leadeth me" means that we have to let go of something or someone we've held dear, He will make it clear that it's time. If we stay sensitive to His Spirit, we'll feel it. We may not *want* to feel it, but it will be undeniable. He'll nudge us to loosen our grip, and if we ask for help, He'll give us just what we need to follow through. He doesn't promise that letting go will be easy, but He does promise that He'll be with us every step. And in the end, we'll likely discover that, in the process, we've learned to hold even more tightly to Him. So the question for us will always be: *Will we trust Him?* Will we trust that the new freedom He's calling us into is far greater than what He's asking us to leave behind? Will we let Him do what He does best, leading us to become more and more like Christ, even when we don't always understand His ways? If we do, we may find great comfort in knowing that we are always led by a loving hand.

Lord, open my heart and loosen my grip!
Help me to focus on the freedom You're calling me into
and let go of whatever hinders me from following You fully.
Thank You for leading me with a loving hand,
and thank You for Your patience and grace
as I learn to walk with You each day. I trust that
You know exactly what I need right now and what I don't.
When it's hard to understand Your ways,
help me to trust Your heart above all.
You are my loving Guide, and there's nowhere I'd rather be
than with You on this journey. May I always know
the comfort of Your presence and the assurance of Your love.

AMEN.

IN CHRIST THERE IS NO EAST OR WEST

CARRY EACH OTHER'S BURDENS,
AND IN THIS WAY YOU WILL
FULFILL THE LAW OF CHRIST.
GALATIANS 6:2 NIV

How many times have you heard the phrase, "I just can't imagine . . ."? We might use those words when we hear a story of life experience so foreign to us that we have a hard time putting ourselves in their shoes. On the flip side, there are things *we* will go through in our lives that others can't fully understand because they haven't walked the same road. Our life paths are as unique as our fingerprints; this is why the reality of *compassion* is vital to living in God's kingdom. In order to love one another well, we must know how to care for one another well. But in order to do *that*, we need to understand each other's struggles as deeply as we can.

The word "compassion" comes from two Latin words: *pati* (to suffer) and *com* (with). To have true compassion for our neighbor is not about feeling sorry for them or wishing that things could be different in their life, but to show up and walk through uncertain or difficult times together. To "suffer with" them, in a sense. To actually be present, listening and doing our best to understand what they truly need. We can help lift a burden, check in with daily encouragement, or ask for specific ways we might support them with prayer or our presence. We can live the beautiful truth of Jesus's message: "Truly I tell you, whatever you did for one of the least of these brothers and sisters of Mine, you did for Me" (Matthew 25:40 NIV).

The hymn "In Christ There Is No East or West" speaks of that soul-deep unity we experience as we serve each other in His Name:

In Him shall true hearts ev'rywhere
Their high communion find;
His service is the golden cord
Close binding all mankind.

Helping to carry someone through life's trials or transitions can bless us deeply and remind us of the vital part we play in bringing God's kingdom to earth. And when it's *our* turn to walk through a rough place on the journey, let's remember to be open to the loving care that our brothers and sisters offer us too. Remember how it can bless them to be on the giving end and how it can help them learn to love others well. Most importantly, they may be reaching out to us in response to the Holy Spirit's nudge—so who are we to argue? Life will ebb and flow as long as we are in this world, doing our best to live in community and follow Jesus. Sometimes we'll be the ones with the opportunity to show compassion, and other times that compassion will be an outpouring of our Father's love for us via those we share our lives with. Think of it! No matter what we go through, we are never alone. Not only can we count on the presence of our loving God, but we can trust Him to send caring hearts our way to love us through anything.

Heavenly Father, what an incredible privilege
it is to be part of Your kingdom on earth.
I want to keep alert for others who need support on the journey.
Help me to deeply understand those
You call me to serve and also show up for them in ways that
truly make a difference. When I am the one in need,
may I be open to the blessing of their care.

AMEN.

EVERLASTING ARMS

Whether we grew up in small towns, bustling, big-city neighborhoods, or in the country, we've all experienced the bittersweet march of time in our own way. All those familiar little shops on Main Street being replaced, one by one, by the new and different . . . or those favorite cafés turning from quaint hangouts to moneymaking franchises seemingly overnight. Bike trails added, old parks taken away. Our little worlds transform before our eyes, whether we want them to or not. That familiar expression "Out with the old, in with the new" brings mixed feelings as we sense the excitement of what is to come mingling with the nostalgia of the past slipping through our fingers. While we can be sentimental souls who have a hard time letting go of what and who we've loved, our longing to hold on to the familiar may also have a lot to do with fearing the unknown.

Of course, we know that time belongs to our Creator. It's not ours to own or control, only to experience as we pass through this wondrous life on earth. It's really hard sometimes, though, when those things, people, and places we hold dear are taken out of our lives before we're ready. We've all felt that sense of insecurity in some way. We know that change is inevitable; none of us can predict what will happen tomorrow, and we find ourselves looking for something solid and lasting to lean on. The words of assurance in the much-loved hymn "Leaning on the Everlasting Arms" have comforted Christians for decades:

What have I to dread, what have I to fear,
Leaning on the everlasting arms?
I have blessed peace with my Lord so near,
Leaning on the everlasting arms.

People in every era have faced their own version of transition—changes in relationships and environments, economic shifts, cultural landscapes. We're all affected by time and progress in some way, every day. When we find ourselves unsettled or we enter a season of big shifts in life (planned or unplanned!), it's wonderful to remember that we're not alone in those feelings. Every human on the planet has experienced it. But there's one thing that sets us apart as followers of Christ in those moments and it is simply this: *we are held— eternally.* There's no tidal wave of transition or change allowed to shake us or steal our peace. Sure, sometimes we allow ourselves to be swept up in fear or beat down by dread, but that's not who we truly are in Him. No matter what is happening around or within us, let's remember that "in Him we live and move and have our being" (Acts 17:28 NIV). He *was* in our beginning, He *is* today, and He *will be* tomorrow. And while we may grieve the loss of what we've held dear and feel uncertain about what is to come, it's a gift to know that we are held through it all in those everlasting arms.

Jesus, Your arms are always open,
and that makes all the difference in the world to me.
No matter what I'm going through, there You are,
offering assurance and giving me a place to rest.
Help me to turn toward You during times of change.
Thank You for Your comfort, encouragement, and,
most of all, the gift of Your unchanging love.

AMEN.

GREAT IS THY FAITHFULNESS

LET ME HEAR OF YOUR UNFAILING LOVE
EACH MORNING, FOR I AM TRUSTING YOU.
SHOW ME WHERE TO WALK, FOR I GIVE MYSELF TO YOU.
PSALM 143:8 NLT

If you've ever watched a sunrise, you know that the transition from night to day can be breathtaking. As light begins to spill out from the darkness, you can see and hear creation slowly awakening all around you. Some people make it a point to watch the sun come up on each birthday they celebrate, signifying the beginning of a new year of life.

Even when we're not witnessing the change firsthand, the idea of morning can be so life-giving that it's impossible to deny our wiring for that kind of hope. Morning is the new start we can look forward to, no matter how we're feeling when our head hits the pillow at night. If today somehow went south—maybe we wish we'd made a different decision or could take back that thing we said or been less anxious or more productive—we know tomorrow brings the chance to do things differently. Tomorrow brings the possibility of seeing life in a new light. What feels hopeless tonight can be transformed by morning, but only if we're willing to let go of it. When we surrender our disappointments and wish-we-could-do-overs to our heavenly Father, we make room for Him to do something new.

In the Bible, the Hebrew word *boqer* is the most commonly used word for "morning," describing "the breaking forth of the dawn" and, more poetically, "bright joy after a night of distress." It's a rhythm we find throughout God's Word and in our own lives. The dark times often precede the most beautiful revelations. The psalmist reminds us that, "Weeping may endure for a night, but joy comes in the morning" (Psalm 30:5 NKJV). Joy is possible from the moment we open our eyes, even before anything is resolved or new plans are made. The next time we wake up and feel yesterday's clouds threatening to roll in, we can remember the One whose mercies are new every morning, the One who has never left our side. We can step into a new day with an awareness of His presence and a sense of hope and assurance. As the hymn "Great Is Thy Faithfulness" reminds us:

> *Pardon for sin and a peace that endureth,*
> *Thine own dear presence to cheer and to guide;*
> *Strength for today and bright hope for tomorrow,*
> *Blessings all mine, with ten thousand beside!*

Our Maker is always at work bringing His light into our lives, offering us renewal and the chance to start again. Whether it's those daily "try-again" moments or ones of lasting transformation, we can be sure that good things are ahead.

Lord, whatever this day brings, I know that it is not mine
to carry into tomorrow. Every day You give us is a chance to
start again, and I never want to take that for granted.
When I lay my head on my pillow tonight, help me remember
that You are here with me, willing to take away
my burdens and prepare me for a new beginning.
Help me to lay it all in Your hands—my doubts and
disappointments, fears and failures. And when I wake up,
remind me of Your mercies that are new every morning.
Thank You for being a faithful, grace-filled God.
Thank You for the beautiful rhythm of Your creation, for always
bringing light from darkness, drawing our hearts toward hope
and renewal and giving us glimpses of Your radiant love.

AMEN.

IN THE GARDEN

FOR AS THE SOIL MAKES THE SPROUT COME UP
AND A GARDEN CAUSES SEEDS TO GROW,
SO THE SOVEREIGN LORD WILL MAKE RIGHTEOUSNESS
AND PRAISE SPRING UP BEFORE ALL NATIONS.
ISAIAH 61:11 NIV

Imagine walking through a beautiful garden, taking in all the colors and marveling at the growth surrounding you. Maybe you're discovering rows of ripe vegetables or fruit trees, each bearing its own form of goodness to delight your taste buds. Or perhaps you're strolling through a fragrant flower garden, selecting your favorite blooms from dozens of exquisite varieties. Gardens have been cherished and celebrated since the beginning of time. From Genesis to Revelation, the Bible is full of nature's beauty, and for good reason! Many of us find peace in the natural world, feeling a connection to our Creator and coming away with a sense of renewal after spending time in His presence there. As the writer of the much-loved hymn "In the Garden" expresses:

I come to the garden alone,

While the dew is still on the roses;

And the voice I hear, Falling on my ear,

The Son of God discloses.

The Lord obviously speaks to the heart through the beauty that surrounds us. But it's easy to forget that, at one time, all the wonders we behold had not appeared but were instead contained in the tiniest seeds! Those seeds were scattered (either naturally or by a human hand), watered, and warmed by the sun, finally finding their way to the surface to bloom and grow into what we see today. No one would ever guess what those little vessels of wonderment would become just by looking at them. So much is orchestrated inside them, unseen, transforming their simple beginning into something unexpectedly marvelous.

Our lives are very much like those seeds, held in the hands of our Creator. Making all things new is His specialty (see Revelation 21:5). Like a master gardener, He knows exactly what wonders will be springing up from our days, even during those times when we doubt anything possibly turning out for our good. What we often see as ordinary, He sees as opportunity. What we see as an ending, He sees as a new start. He sees the potential in the little things we overlook—the everyday interactions, seemingly unimportant moments, and even the times of prayer when we just aren't feelin' it. He is always up to something good.

As we surrender our days to Him, we create space for Him to show up in His way, in His time, to fill our lives with the kind of beauty and joy that only He can provide. Most of us have learned that it's an "inside job" anyway. We know that our attempts to control our circumstances or striving to arrange the life we *think* will make us perpetually happy are futile. Sure, we can choose to do more of what makes us smile. We can surround ourselves with good things and people who speak to our heart. But ultimately, just like what happens within those seeds, God is up to something bigger, truer, and deeper than we could ever know. And the best part is, He's here to enjoy it all with us, as our ever-present companion on the journey.

Lord, what beauty You have grown around and within us!
Thank You for all the ways You show up like a gardener . . .
planting, nurturing, and even pruning those things in my life
that You're bringing to fruition. Help me trust that You are
always doing that good work within me even when I can't see it.
And whenever I look around at Your magnificent creation,
may my heart turn toward You in awe and gratitude.

AMEN.

COME, THOU FOUNT OF EVERY BLESSING

THEN SAMUEL TOOK A STONE AND SET IT UP BETWEEN MIZPAH AND SHEN AND CALLED ITS NAME EBENEZER; FOR HE SAID, "TILL NOW THE LORD HAS HELPED US."

I SAMUEL 7:12 ESV

Think about a time you experienced a big transition or faced a significant shift in your life. It may have been an unwanted change or one you saw as good and helpful (those kinds have their share of adjustments and challenges too!). Did you wonder how you would possibly get through it? Whether we view change as positive or negative, it is rarely easy—and it may take a while to find our footing once we get to the other side of the episode. Have you ever stopped to look back at the beginning of it all and thought, *Did that really just happen? What a journey! How in the world did I make it through?*

As God's children, we recognize that it isn't the world successfully bringing us through these times. We know it's Him, in all kinds of ways—guiding us by bringing people into our lives, orchestrating circumstances, or providing holy nudges and His heart-lifting words of encouragement. We can trust that He not only allowed the journey we just took, but He used it for our good in ways we probably aren't even aware of yet. One of the most important things we can do on the other side of it all is to *remember*. Remember how this transition felt in the beginning, how He showed up (sometimes in the least-expected ways!), and how generously He blessed us along the journey.

Many of us have heard the term "Ebenezer," referring to the stone that was set up by the Hebrew prophet Samuel to commemorate the help God had given the Israelites. Samuel knew it was important not only to express his thanks but to remember what God had done—and to remind His people too. We humans can be a forgetful bunch, and the more often we remind ourselves (and one another) of how God provides, the less fear we'll have about the next leg of the journey. We know that He has shown Himself faithful and that we can count on Him to be there again. The story we tell about our journey can be our "Ebenezer." We can assure ourselves and others that the road ahead will be marked with more altars of remembrance, because He will never stop showing up for us. As the hymn "Come, Thou Fount of Every Blessing" reminds us:

> *Here I raise my Ebenezer;*
> *Here by Thy great help I've come;*
> *And I hope, by Thy good pleasure,*
> *Safely to arrive at home.*

As Christians, we believe we're pilgrims passing through this world. We are headed somewhere unspeakably glorious, but we have good work to do on the way. Let's share our stories of how God has shown up for us on the journey, in good times and in bad. We need to remember how it felt to overcome against the odds, to wonder how we were going to make it and have God carry us through. We can all use a reminder now and then that we will never walk alone.

Lord, I am so grateful for all You have done. When I remember all the ways You've shown up for me, it gives me courage for the road ahead. You know what I need before I ask, and You never leave my side. Remind me often of all we have walked through together, and bring others into my life who may need support on their journey. I will speak of Your love and faithfulness as often as I'm able. Help me to always trust You for the next step— and to encourage my brothers and sisters to do the same.

AMEN.

HOW FIRM A FOUNDATION

FOR NO ONE CAN LAY ANY FOUNDATION
OTHER THAN THE ONE WE ALREADY HAVE—
JESUS CHRIST.
I CORINTHIANS 3:11 NLT

Retirement is one of those elusive milestones we may not often think about when we're younger (besides some early financial planning!), but as we get older, we begin to realize that it's not as far down the road as we thought. Today, retiring can look very different than it used to. For many, it's not a permanent vacation. Images of endless days lounging at the beach or on the couch are replaced by continued activity of some kind. Of course, pursuing lifelong dreams, taking up hobbies, and traveling are all part of that, but a lot of people continue to find purpose in some kind of work. They may volunteer or find another job after leaving their "real" one, whether out of necessity, the desire to serve, or the need to feel like they still have some kind of significance. Regardless, one of the greatest challenges many retired people face is letting go of what has been a big part of their identity. The role they filled, their work relationships, even the routine they may have had for years—it all changes, and that can make a person feel a little (or a lot!) disoriented. Unfortunately, our culture doesn't help much with this stage in life. Its obsession with youth and the fear of growing older or less "relevant" can make people feel hesitant about aging and all that comes with it. The classic hymn "How Firm a Foundation" reminds us that, as Christians, we have a solid place to stand no matter what we're going through. We have a purpose that transcends any job title or sense of identity. It began when we came to know Christ, and it exists for all eternity. We live to glorify God and share the love He has given us through His Son:

> *E'en down to old age all My people shall prove*
> *My sovereign, eternal, unchangeable love;*
> *And then, when grey hairs shall their temples adorn,*
> *Like lambs they shall still in My bosom be borne.*

Even if we haven't yet reached retirement age, it's never too early to strengthen our identity in Christ. The more firmly we are rooted in Him, believing what He says about us instead of what the world proclaims, the less our transitions will shake us—because we know who we are, why we're here, and where we're headed. We can rest assured that whatever happens on the way can never change that glorious truth.

> *Lord, help me to remember that I am Yours at every age.*
> *You're the One in whom I find my truest identity,*
> *and nothing will ever change who I am in You.*
> *I lift up anyone who may be currently*
> *going through the transition of retirement.*
> *I pray they'll be reminded that*
> *the world will never truly determine their worth—*
> *only You can do that.*
> *Thank You for being our firm foundation,*
> *no matter what we experience in life.*
> *May I always live out my purpose*
> *as a vessel for Your love.*

AMEN.

HIS EYE IS ON THE SPARROW

ARE NOT TWO SPARROWS SOLD FOR A PENNY?
YET NOT ONE OF THEM WILL FALL TO THE GROUND
OUTSIDE YOUR FATHER'S CARE.
MATTHEW 10:29 NIV

Some of the most significant changes we'll experience in life may never be known to anyone else. That's because they happen *within* us, and they may just be beyond words . . . which is perfectly okay, because there's truly only One who needs to know what's going on with us, and He already does. He sees us from every angle and understands the heart more deeply than anyone else ever could.

Our inner changes may be some kind of emotional healing or maybe a letting go of an attitude or negative belief about ourselves that we've held on to for years. They may involve the significant decision to finally forgive someone or repent of something that has weighed upon us and stolen our joy for far too long. Regardless, here's a wonderful truth we can cling to amid everything: when the Holy Spirit brings about these shifts within us, He doesn't leave us halfway through the process—He's with us all the way. That's a reassuring thought because although transformation is a wonderful thing, it doesn't generally happen at lightning speed . . . and it can feel more like surgery before it feels like healing. God knows change isn't easy for us, but He also knows that the joy of our becoming more like Christ is more than worth the temporary discomfort it takes to get there.

So when you sense His Spirit nudging you toward inner change, what should you do? Here are two simple but powerful suggestions: *pray* and *praise*. First, begin to pray specifically about what He might be drawing your attention toward. If He's up to something big in your heart, He'll make it known in His way and in His time. Your job is merely to pay attention. Second: praise. Whatever you are experiencing, realize that you have a Father who cares so deeply about you that every detail about you matters to Him. He will never stop searching your heart for anything that would come between you and your freedom in Christ. Even on the days you aren't feeling it, when you shift your heart toward gratitude for all He has done, it will lift your spirit, renew your perspective, and remind you of how precious you are to Him. Just think—there are billions of human beings on this planet, and He has His loving eye on each of us as if there were only one of us. Just as we sing in "His Eye Is on the Sparrow":

I sing because I'm happy,
I sing because I'm free,
For His eye is on the sparrow,
And I know He watches me.

Nothing about us is too small or insignificant for our Creator to care for. His redeeming love doesn't miss a detail. And just as Jesus reminds His disciples in Matthew 10:31 as He sends them out into the world, "You are worth more than many sparrows," so, too, can we count on the Father's constant care, because we are infinitely precious to Him. No matter what's going on inside us, He is beside us, within and without, closer than our next breath, working in ways we can't even imagine in order to bring about our wholeness in Him.

Lord, what an indescribable gift to know that I am forever held
in Your loving gaze and that You care so deeply about every
detail of my life. You see more clearly into my heart than
anyone can—You created it! You know exactly what I need
as I experience inner change. Help me to hear Your voice
and to be willing to do whatever You ask in order
to live more fully and freely in Christ.

AMEN.

HIS EYE IS
ON THE SPARROW

Why should I feel discouraged,
Why should the shadows come,
Why should my heart be lonely,
And long for heav'n and home,
When Jesus is my portion?
My constant friend is He:
His eye is on the sparrow,
And I know He watches me;
His eye is on the sparrow,
And I know He watches me.

I sing because I'm happy,
I sing because I'm free,
For His eye is on the sparrow,
And I know He watches me.

"Let not your heart be troubled,"
His tender word I hear,
And resting on His goodness,
I lose my doubts and fears;
Though by the path He leadeth,
But one step I may see;
His eye is on the sparrow,
And I know He watches me;
His eye is on the sparrow,
And I know He watches me.

Whenever I am tempted,
Whenever clouds arise;
When songs give place to sighing,
When hope within me dies,
I draw the closer to Him,
From care He sets me free;
His eye is on the sparrow,
And I know He watches me;
His eye is on the sparrow,
And I know He watches me.

TRUST AND OBEY

Oh, those busy seasons in our lives . . . they can be tough to navigate. We catch ourselves saying things like, "As soon as . . ." or "When I get around to it . . ." or "One of these days . . . ." You know, the phrases that can get us off the hook a little while longer when everything's coming at us at once? There can be so much vying for our attention that it's hard to know where to begin. We have our short-term to-do-lists, our long-term goals, things other people need from us, things the media reminds us that we *should* be prioritizing—where do we even start?

Some of us are masters at getting right to it. We're *pre*–crastinators. We can't rest until we've checked off everything on that list and hopefully before noon. We're the ones who remind people that "Someday" isn't a day of the week. *You need to Carpe Diem! Get a planner, get a life coach, and make things happen while you can!* But others are the better-known *procrastinators*. We know what needs to be done, but for whatever reason, we just don't wanna . . . and so we find all the reasons we can't right now. *Yes, that big thing is important, but so are these ten other little things that popped up today.* The list gets longer, the priorities get confused, we feel overwhelmed a lot, and we just can't figure out how to get it together. Of course, many of us fall somewhere in between those extremes, just doing our best to take care of ourselves and our families and trying to keep as many plates spinning as we can.

If we want to find some measure of peace in the busyness, it's vital that we come away from time to time to check in with our Maker. What would He put at the top of the list right now? What need is He drawing our attention to? What is He asking us to lay down, and what new thing might He be calling us to consider instead? It takes time to sit and get quiet to hear from Him. But *it is so worth it*. What we're doing in those moments is saying with our heart: *I trust You with my life. I need You to show me the way*. The song "Trust and Obey" speaks of the peace and assurance that can fill our lives as we learn to lay everything down:

Then in fellowship sweet
We will sit at His feet,
Or we'll walk by His side in the way;
What He says we will do,
Where He sends we will go—
Never fear, only trust and obey.

We humans are masters at creating busyness for ourselves, even as we complain that we're way too busy! Of course, being productive is a wonderful thing, but we'll never enjoy the journey if we always feel as if we're spinning our wheels. Part of trusting Jesus is letting go of those things we do to give ourselves purpose and grabbing hold of His true purpose for us instead. Stopping now and then to hear from Him can make all the difference in the world.

Lord, all my days are in Your hands. As I make lists,
set priorities, and go for those goals that feel important to me,
I need to remember that You're the One who knows what's best.
Help me set aside time to listen to the voice of Your Spirit.
Help me surrender my idea of what is most important and
follow Your lead instead. May I learn to trust You
more and more each day.

AMEN.

I AM JESUS'S LITTLE LAMB

AT THAT TIME THE DISCIPLES CAME TO JESUS
AND ASKED, "WHO, THEN, IS THE GREATEST
IN THE KINGDOM OF HEAVEN?"
HE CALLED A LITTLE CHILD TO HIM,
AND PLACED THE CHILD AMONG THEM.
MATTHEW 18:1–2 NIV

Do you know who can be some of our greatest teachers during times of change? Kids. If you've ever observed young children reacting to new things, you've probably witnessed some of the following: excitement, wonder, curiosity, joy, a sense of adventure, and the kind of childlike faith that makes us wish we could be five again. Of course, Jesus knows our humanness inside and out. He knows that as we grow older, it's easy to collect worries, become overcautious, and live with more anxiety about what's to come but less delight in the present moment. He witnesses our tendency to overcomplicate, overthink, and overanalyze. He sees where that gets us—far from our heart and stuck in our head.

When He took the little children into His arms and said that the "kingdom of God belongs to such as these" (Luke 18:16 NIV), He was calling the world (that means us!) to pay attention. He saw the splendor in kids' simplicity. He knew that the lens through which they look at life is precious and fleeting, their hearts not yet closed to possibility and their minds not so clouded with judgment. Kids tend to be more resilient in times of transition because they haven't started to try to control it all. They still live with that natural ability to look for the good and roll with the rest. Sure, there can be some whining and worrying involved, but there's an openness that many adults don't possess—a willingness to give things a try to see what happens. That's one powerful way God can show up for us at any age, in the space created by our childlike faith. When we encounter new opportunities, we can choose to close the door quickly to avoid the unknown or we can remain open, praying for the simple trust needed to take a chance. Sure, we're all grown up now, but that doesn't mean we have to give up dependence on our Father. We just need to be reminded that we're still very much His children—no matter how many years pass—and that He delights in providing for us in every way. The hymn "I Am Jesus's Little Lamb" is a sweet reminder of that ageless connection:

> I am Jesus's little lamb,
> Ever glad at heart I am;
> For my Shepherd gently guides me,
> Knows my need and well provides me.

So the next time we're prayerfully considering a new opportunity, let's remember that we have the best of both worlds *now*—the kid in us who can frame it up as a faith-filled adventure and the adult who can use the wisdom we've gained through the years—as God guides us through. What a gift to know that we'll never outgrow the tenderness of His love.

Lord, I want to live with childlike faith again!
I want to place that simple trust in You that comes so naturally
to little ones. Help me learn to live more and more with
an open heart and mind, to let go of trying to control so much,
and to face life's changes with less fear and more acceptance.
Help me find joy in trying new things—
and always remember that You are with me in all I do.
You hold my life in Your hands.

AMEN.

TO GOD BE THE GLORY

FOR FROM HIM AND THROUGH HIM
AND FOR HIM ARE ALL THINGS.
TO HIM BE THE GLORY FOREVER! AMEN.
ROMANS 11:36 NIV

We humans are drawn to new experiences for many different reasons. Some of us are thrill seekers, inspired by big adventures and unique challenges. Others are lifelong learners, curious about the world around us, always wanting to know and understand more about this remarkable life we've been given. Some of us have a sense of wanderlust from an early age and we'll take any opportunity we can to travel . . . anywhere! Then, there are those who have learned to look for undiscovered delights right in their own cities, towns, and backyards.

When we keep our eyes, mind, and heart open, there's no telling what we might discover. One of the most mind-blowing things about this universe we inhabit is that everything at which we marvel—every new experience we encounter or journey we embark upon—is a reflection of the magnificence of our Creator. It may be just a glimmer of His glory, but the moments that steal our heart and speak to our soul are like arrows pointing to Him. The beauty of our natural world, the unexpected blessings that make us smile and warm our heart, the unforgettable times that take our breath away . . . these are little tastes of the glory we were made for all along. When we find ourselves caught up in those moments, we can find joy in remembering the One who provided them. Remember, He doesn't surprise and delight us just to make us happy (though that is wonderful in itself!). But even more than that, He is offering the gift of Himself in new ways. He's giving us glimpses of His heart for us, opportunities that are tailor-made for connecting with Him in a way that only we can. He knows how we're wired, and He knows just what captures our heart and fills us with joy and wonder. And, of course, the greatest gift He offers us is Jesus Himself. Life in Christ is the ultimate adventure. No matter what we experience in this world, we know that what is to come is infinitely greater because of Him. The hymn "To God Be the Glory" reminds us:

> *Great things He hath taught us, great things He hath done,*
> *And great our rejoicing through Jesus the Son;*
> *But purer, and higher, and greater will be*
> *Our wonder, our transport, when Jesus we see.*

So no matter what new endeavors we embark upon or discoveries we make, let's remember the One who is drawing us to Himself through it all. What a beautiful truth to carry in our heart no matter what we experience. We may catch those glimmers of glory on earth, but the One who is "the image of the invisible God, the firstborn over all creation" (Colossians 1:15 NIV) lives within us and is with us in everything we do. What more could we wish for than that?

Loving Creator, there are so many wonderful facets of You!
I want to see You in every new opportunity I'm given,
every awe-inspiring discovery I make,
and every unexpected blessing I receive.
Help me to see life with You as an adventure.
Thank You for Jesus and the countless ways He reflects
Your heart for us. No matter what happens in this life,
I know that the greatest moments I'll ever experience
will be in His presence.

AMEN.

TURN YOUR EYES UPON JESUS

*COME WITH ME BY YOURSELVES
TO A QUIET PLACE AND GET SOME REST.*
MARK 6:31 NIV

If you tend to be an overthinker, change may feel extra overwhelming to you. We overthinkers have an incredible ability to add many complicated layers to a situation by the stories we tell ourselves about it, the fears that spring up out of nowhere, and the whole host of anxious thoughts that run rampant on the hamster wheels of our mind. It can feel like a part-time job just managing all that while we're walking through any transition in life. Jesus was clearly aware of our common human condition when He walked among us, often addressing the worries of the people and redirecting their thoughts from fear to faith. And the beautiful and brilliant thing about the way He did that was the simplicity of it. Anyone, anywhere, can do what He's inviting us to do: *just turn your eyes toward Me*. The beloved hymn "Turn Your Eyes upon Jesus" reminds us of His invitation:

Turn your eyes upon Jesus,
Look full in His wonderful face,
And the things of earth will grow strangely dim,
In the light of His glory and grace.

We live in a time of information overload. We're constantly bombarded with solutions to problems we didn't even know we had. Perhaps we make lists and collect ideas for how to do things better, to find more balance, or to navigate life's changes successfully. But the truth is, while all those things can be helpful, they'll never do what a quiet moment in God's presence can do. When we are experiencing something new and unfamiliar, it can be easy to panic and grasp for whatever will bring a sense of safety and assurance. And while the world has plenty of solutions, the Father has one: *Jesus*. Our Light, our Shepherd, Our Prince of Peace awaits our company every moment of the day. Like Martha, busy in the kitchen, we often allow His quiet invitation to be drowned out by the urgency we feel to be productive. But like Mary, we too can pause in the midst of whatever we're experiencing and sit at His feet for a few moments. We can take a breath and shift our focus away from our overrun mind and toward a simple thought of Him. We can become aware of His presence and be reminded of His promised provision and unconditional love.

To sum it up, we can just simply *be*. Simple answers aren't so popular these days. We're expected to buy the book, watch the video, or follow the social media thread to happiness. What the Father has provided in His Son is available to any of us at any moment, no strings attached. Give it a try the next time your mind is filled with worry. Just sit awhile in His presence until you feel His peace.

Lord, it's easy to get caught up in the things
that distract me from being with You.
Thank You for Your daily invitation
to rest at Your feet whenever I need it.
Thank You for the gift of Your loyal and unconditional love,
especially when I enter uncharted territory
and need the extra assurance that it's all going to be okay.
I want to return to You often to savor
Your presence and keep my eyes on You,
no matter what this life brings.

AMEN.

THE MARRIAGE SUPPER

AND THE ANGEL SAID TO ME, "WRITE THIS:
BLESSED ARE THOSE WHO ARE INVITED
TO THE MARRIAGE SUPPER OF THE LAMB."
REVELATION 19:9 ESV

Weddings can be such beautiful reflections of God's heart for us. If you've ever watched the father of the bride help to prepare for a wedding, you've likely witnessed some real love in action. Of course every experience is different, but even if we haven't had the gift of our own father figure in our lives, most of us have witnessed a loving father preparing to give his little girl away. In the days leading up to the big event, a dad can often be found behind the scenes doing such unglamorous duties as errand-running, check-writing, and taxi-driving while brides and their moms may be arranging flowers, going to brunch, or getting pedicures. (Yes, parents do lots of other things too, but let's give those oft-overlooked dads a little credit!) There may be a reception tent to set up or some loose wires to fix or a million tiny lights to put in place before morning. Who's there with the duct tape, ladder, and loads of reassurance? Dad. He's emotional (even if he doesn't show it), protective (it's a good thing that husband of hers asked permission!), and above all, he's happy, even through tears, to know that his daughter is starting a new life with someone who cherishes her. This is such a touching illustration of our heavenly Father, too, who lovingly works behind the scenes to bring us new life in Christ. Why does He do it all—caring about every little detail and showing up in those unexpected ways that only He can? Because He treasures us so completely, like that father on his daughter's wedding day. The Lord delights in helping us embark upon the greatest adventure of our lives, an eternal relationship with His Son. Revelation 19:6–8 offers a heartwarming glimpse of the church celebrating that long-awaited union with Christ: "Let us rejoice and exult and give him the glory, for the marriage of the Lamb has come, and his Bride has made herself ready" (ESV). In the joyful hymn "The Marriage Supper," we sing:

> *O the bride shall shine in bright array,*
> *With her tears all forever wiped away;*
> *There will be a great rejoicing on that day,*
> *At the great marriage supper of the Lamb.*

As we imagine that scene, we may think of the inexplicable joy we will feel as guests at that table. But what about the Father who orchestrated it all? The One who has been preparing us for this new beginning since our very first breath? Can you imagine *His* joy? Can you imagine the love that must fill His heart, having brought all His daughters and sons from every tribe, tongue, and nation—from the beginning of time to that moment of eternal union with Christ? It's so good to remember how much He delights in us, simply because we are *His*, not because we have earned it. And like that earthly behind-the-scenes wedding dad, our heavenly Father surely awaits our union with great anticipation.

Father God, thank You for all the ways we can see
Your heart reflected in the loving fathers we know.
What an incredible gift it is to know that You delight
in each of us just because we are Yours!
May we be reminded often of all You have done
and all that You do today to bring us new life in Christ.
As we anticipate that eternal celebration with You,
help us savor Your love in new ways every day.
You are all we will ever need.

AMEN.

AT THE NAME OF JESUS

AND YOU ARE TO GIVE HIM THE NAME JESUS,
BECAUSE HE WILL SAVE HIS PEOPLE
FROM THEIR SINS.
MATTHEW 1:21 NIV

"What's in a name?" You may have heard this old Shakespearean quote at some point in your life. It's a question that packs a punch. And although Romeo and Juliet may have had a different take on it, the truth is that there can be a whole *lot* in a name! Something new and transformative happens when we ascribe a name to something or someone. First, we are acknowledging their existence. We are saying, "I see you." We're also honoring their uniqueness: "Not only do I see you, but I recognize that there is no one else exactly like you in all of creation." And finally, we are signifying a relationship: "By giving you this name, I am creating a deeper connection between us."

Of course, it all goes back to Genesis 2: "Out of the ground the LORD God formed every beast of the field and every bird of the air, and brought them to Adam to see what he would call them" (NKJV). Adam's naming of the animals gave them a new kind of significance. And when he named "woman," he acknowledged a relationship so deep that they were "one flesh." Fast forward many, many years and think of new parents in hospitals today who are gazing lovingly at their newborn baby and speaking that carefully chosen name for the first time in his or her young life. It's likely that name has a very special meaning to the couple, and their child now brings new life to it. Then we could think of names we acquired throughout our life. Nicknames often spring up in families or among friends as signs of affection or inside jokes that endear us to one another. It warms our heart when someone feels close enough to claim us as their own in a very personal way. But of course, the ultimate example of "what's in a name" is found in Jesus. His Name alone represents all we could ever need. As Paul declares in Philippians 2:9, "Therefore God has highly exalted him and bestowed on him the name that is above every name" (ESV). The hymn "At the Name of Jesus" celebrates that truth:

> *At the name of Jesus, ev'ry knee shall bow,*
> *Ev'ry tongue confess Him King of glory now.*
> *'Tis the Father's pleasure we should call Him Lord,*
> *Who from the beginning was the mighty Word.*

One way the Bible reveals God's nature is through the many facets of His Son. Jesus is called our Advocate, Bread of Life, Deliverer, Mediator, Shepherd, Redeemer, Rock . . . and the list goes on. As we dig into the meaning of those titles and consider all He means to us, we are drawn closer to Him. And we can be sure that He, in turn, knows the meaning of *us*, unlike anyone else ever has or will. Regardless of what our name means to anyone on earth, it means something wonderful to Him because He has claimed us as His own. As the Father so lovingly reminds us in Isaiah 43:1: "Fear not, for I have redeemed you; I have called you by name, you are mine" (ESV).

Lord, You are infinitely greater than we could ever find words
for, but You have made a way for us to understand You
more deeply through language. I am so grateful for that gift.
May I always delight in discovering new facets of You,
and may Your Name often be on my lips in praise and gratitude.

AMEN.

GOD OMNISCIENT

I'M AN OPEN BOOK TO YOU;
EVEN FROM A DISTANCE,
YOU KNOW WHAT I'M THINKING.
PSALM 139:2 THE MESSAGE

New ideas—we all have them. We may get excited and want to share them with the world, or we may feel self-conscious, wondering who would actually believe that we have something significant to contribute. After all, no one else can fully understand our own idea the way we can because it begins in our own mind and heart! And unless we find the courage to flesh it out and move it forward, that's where it will remain. If we've committed to following Jesus, then we must consider that any good gift we're given could be for more than just *our* benefit. It may be something for us to share with those around us too. And that includes our ideas! Whether it be in our home, our community, the medical field, creative arts, faith organizations—the list can go on—that idea rising up in us may be much more purposeful than we realize. Some of the world's most life-giving organizations, inventions, and endeavors have been started by someone who felt a nudge from the Creator—someone who knew they had been given something not only for themselves but also to bless those around them. That realization gave them the courage to step out and go for it. How quickly we can forget what we are capable of in Christ!

The world often reminds us of how inadequate we are under our own power—how we need this or that platform or a specific endorsement or marketing trick should we want to be "successful." But our faithful Father reminds us that the world isn't running the show. He's the One who blesses us with the ideas we have and the abilities and opportunities we need to see those ideas through.

It's not about finding some loophole or orchestrating the perfect connection to make ourselves heard. *Yes*, it's important to make the effort to follow through in all the practical ways we can. And, *yes*, those connections are wonderful and often provided by Him. But in the end, He is the One who already sees it from beginning to end. *Omniscience* (meaning "all-knowing") is a word that sounds a little archaic these days, but it is absolutely who He was, is, and always will be. The hymn "God Omniscient" reminds us of this truth:

> *God of love, God of light,*
> *Guide my trusting soul aright;*
> *God of wisdom, God of pow'r,*
> *Be Thou with me ev'ry hour.*

With all the influences around us, it can sometimes be hard to believe that there's an underlying wisdom and power that is infinitely greater than anything our human mind can fathom. But it's true! When something new bubbles up for us, it may very well be a gift to the world from the Holy Spirit dwelling within us—which means that what we do with that idea matters greatly, no matter how big or small it seems. Our job is simply to offer it to Him, open ourselves up to possibilities, and see what He has in store. It may not at all play out like we imagine. It could end up being an opportunity to trust Him more or be a stepping-stone to something else. Or it could be something the world has never seen.

Lord, Your wisdom is infinite. When an idea comes to me,
even the smallest seed of an idea, remind me to offer it to You.
No matter what happens, I pray that my thoughts and actions
will bring You glory, and I thank You for allowing me
to have some small part in Your magnificent
and ever-unfolding story.

AMEN.

OPEN MY EYES, THAT I MAY SEE

THE EYE IS THE LAMP OF THE BODY.
SO, IF YOUR EYE IS HEALTHY,
YOUR WHOLE BODY WILL BE FULL OF LIGHT.
MATTHEW 6:22 ESV

Have you ever used the term "new normal" to describe what life feels like after a huge change? Once the letting go has ended and the embracing of something new has begun, it starts to sink in that life for us will never be exactly what it was before. This happens in all sorts of ways—losing a physical ability, adding a child, becoming a full-time caretaker for a loved one, adapting to a new environment, and the list can go on. Even situations that won't last forever can require major long-term adjustments to our routine, our attitude, and our choices. We learn quite a bit about ourselves in those times . . . namely that we find a lot of comfort in familiarity and we often work really hard to keep our lives intact so that we don't have to deal with the upheaval of change. We can be pretty good at it, too, until we're reminded that God will always have more for us to learn and it won't always be comfortable. Whether it's a change we choose to make or one that's thrust upon us, it is inevitable that there is some kind of adaptation in our future. If it hasn't happened lately, it will, and when it does, we would be wise to remember this: *the more we fight to keep things "our way," the more frustrated and disappointed we will become.* During those times of change (and even before they hit!), one of the most freeing things we can do is simply ask our Creator to help us let go. As we loosen our grip on our expectations and attachments, we can celebrate the good we find in each moment. We can open our eyes to the possibilities, the unexpected blessings, and the silver linings. One thing we can be certain of is that if we pay attention, God will always use our circumstances to reveal more of Himself to us. Our part of the experience is to be and remain open, just as the beautiful hymn "Open My Eyes, That I May See" reminds us:

> *Open my eyes, that I may see*
> *Glimpses of truth Thou hast for me.*
> *Place in my hands the wonderful key*
> *That shall unclasp and set me free.*

The less energy we use for trying to keep things as they were yesterday, the more energy we have for embracing life as it is today. And we might as well practice that as often as we can, because life will continually remind us that change is inevitable! People change. Circumstances change. Nature changes. That's something we would do well to remember when the curtain opens on a new scene in life: it's not an interruption; it's an opportunity. Our Maker is already there, wanting to experience it with us and offering us fresh perspectives. We're invited to shed that business-as-usual way we've been living and see it all with new eyes once more.

Father, You are the One who makes all things new, and
I invite You to do that in my life in whatever way is needed.
I don't want to sleepwalk through the years,
clinging to familiarity and comfort,
only to discover that I missed so much on the way.
I know You have wonders in store for us that we can't
even imagine, both here on earth and in our heavenly home.
Open my eyes to it all, that I may live an awakened life.

AMEN.

HOLD TO GOD'S UNCHANGING HAND

FOR WHICH OF YOU, DESIRING TO BUILD A TOWER,
DOES NOT FIRST SIT DOWN AND COUNT THE COST,
WHETHER HE HAS ENOUGH TO COMPLETE IT?
LUKE 14:28 ESV

It seems like construction is going on somewhere near us all the time—maybe a new house in the neighborhood, a section of highway on our route to work, old businesses being torn down, new schools going up. There's a lot happening out there most days! And we usually pass right by the action unless it somehow affects us personally. Workers in the fields of construction, architecture, or engineering have a behind-the-scenes understanding of what it takes to make those transformations happen. Otherwise, we likely have no idea how much up-front planning and hard work goes into it. But we all know that new structures don't spring up overnight, and they certainly don't happen without a detailed plan. Imagine two different kinds of builders. One gets so excited about her new endeavor that she buys some ground, calls a few friends to help, finds some tools that seem like they'd be useful, and starts hammering away at the project. The second type of person lays the groundwork first and then takes the meticulous steps he needs to follow through. Of course, we know the intentional way is the only way to build something that will last. But it takes some patience, discipline, and discernment—three things we humans often struggle with.

It's a great illustration of our faith journey. Some of us can identify a significant time when our new life in Christ began. It can feel like a whole new world when we let go of our old lives and begin a relationship with Him. Even if our circumstances didn't change, our heart was filled with a new kind of hope and our mind was opened to life-giving truths for the first time. It can feel as if we were being rebuilt from the ground up—exciting, exhilarating, and maybe even exhausting. We may rush in, absorb lots of knowledge, make big changes, seek out new relationships and experiences . . . and end up feeling overwhelmed. That's how the first builder feels: excited, inspired, and motivated but ultimately lacking some balance and structure. It's so easy (and so human!) for us to let our emotions lead and then be hard on ourselves when we hit a low point and find ourselves on shaky ground. No matter how long we've been walking with Jesus, it's good to remember to pause once in a while to get our bearings and check in with the Builder of our faith. The hymn "Hold to God's Unchanging Hand" reminds us to do just that:

Time is filled with swift transition.
Naught of earth unmoved can stand.
Build your hopes on things eternal.
Hold to God's unchanging hand.

Is it time to slow down? To let some things go? Or welcome new ways of doing life? Which commitments are serving His purpose and which ones are standing in the way? Asking some simple but prayerful questions now and then can help to recenter us and prepare us for the path ahead. We can always carry the excitement, wonder, and joy in our heart that our life in Christ has brought. But we can also use the wisdom He provides to keep us grounded and growing steadily along the way.

Lord, thank You for being a compassionate and understanding
Father. During those times when I let my feelings lead,
when I feel overwhelmed and a little lost on the journey,
please help me to find my bearings again in You.
I don't ever want to lose the excitement of my life in Christ,
but I want to be intentional about what we're building together.
My mind and heart are Yours.

AMEN.

HOLD TO GOD'S UNCHANGING HAND

Time is filled with swift transition.
Naught of earth unmoved can stand.
Build your hopes on things eternal.
Hold to God's unchanging hand.

Hold to His hand, God's unchanging hand.
Hold to His hand, God's unchanging hand.
Build your hopes on things eternal.
Hold to God's unchanging hand.

Trust in Him who will not leave you.
Whatsoever years may bring.
If by earthly friends forsaken,
Still more closely to Him cling.

Covet not this world's vain riches
That so rapidly decay.
Seek to gain the heav'nly treasures.
They will never pass away.

When your journey is completed,
If to God you have been true,
Fair and bright the home in Glory
Your enraptured soul will view.

ALL THINGS ARE POSSIBLE

I KNOW THAT YOU CAN DO ALL THINGS,
AND THAT NO PLAN IS IMPOSSIBLE FOR YOU.
JOB 42:2 NASB

People often use the phrase "Believe in yourself" to show support for one another, to remind others that it's okay to hope for things, and to help each other through times of discouragement. It can mean the world to a person to know that someone is in their corner who sees their potential and wants them to see it too. As believers in Christ, we can appreciate that loving intention, but we also know that our ultimate Source of strength and provision is not ourselves—it's our God. So when we *do* catch a vision for something, we know that the first and greatest thing we can do is bring it to the Lord in prayer. As most of us have learned in some way, simply because we want to do something with all our heart and it makes perfect sense to us to do it, our Maker can see that big picture of our life, and He knows just how it will (or won't) fit in.

It's like one of those direction apps on a smartphone. We can zoom in on the destination and may see it in vivid detail, but God's broader view tells a much more complete story. He knows it may not be the best thing for us—or perhaps it's not the right timing—and as hard as it is to switch gears, we will never regret heeding that gentle "No" or "Not now" from the Holy Spirit. However, when He *does* give us the green light, nothing can stop us from fulfilling His purposes. "Is anything too difficult for the Lord?" The question is asked in Genesis 18:14 (NASB). And the answer in our heart can be a resounding *No!* with those words of Jesus from Matthew 19:26: "With man this is impossible, but with God all things are possible" (NIV).

We can imagine the writer's conviction as he penned the hopeful hymn "All Things Are Possible":

All things are possible to God,

To Christ, the power of God in man;

To me, when I am all renewed,

When I in Christ am formed again.

So when we hear that well-meaning bit of "Believe in yourself" encouragement, let's remember the things we *can* believe about ourselves: We've been adopted as God's children (Ephesians 1:5); we have the mind of Christ (I Corinthians 2:16); the Holy Spirit lives within us (I Corinthians 6:19); God's angels surround us (Psalm 91:11); the evil one can't touch us (I John 5:18); and we can do all things through Christ who strengthens us (Philippians 4:13) . . . just to name a few! As the hymn reminds us, the truth revealed by Galatians 2:20 changes everything: "My old self has been crucified with Christ. It is no longer I who live, but Christ lives in me. So I live in this earthly body by trusting in the Son of God, who loved me and gave Himself for me" (NLT). That self we are today is worth believing in because we know who we are in Him. We know that we live this life for Him and that nothing we accomplish will be done apart from Him. We can believe in our God-created, Spirit-filled selves because *He* does, and we can trust that anything He calls us to do in this life is possible through Him who gives us all we need to see it through!

Lord, thank You for every good gift You've given us in Christ.
Because of Him, I can live confidently in this world,
trusting that I have all I need to do anything You call me to do.
Every time I look in the mirror, may I be reminded of that truth.
I believe in who You created me to be.

AMEN.

BE STILL, MY SOUL

AND BE SURE OF THIS:
I AM WITH YOU ALWAYS,
EVEN TO THE END OF THE AGE.
MATTHEW 28:20 NLT

If we were given the chance to filter out things from our life experiences, it's likely that some of us would choose to eliminate loss. That word *loss* can refer to a lot of things—for example, having to bid farewell to what is most comforting and familiar to us (even as far back as that favorite baby blanket or teddy bear!), being let go from a meaningful job, parting with a friend who moves away, or ultimately saying goodbye to a dear one who leaves this earth. Throughout our human experience, we will all encounter loss in our own way, and it just doesn't feel right. Something deep within us surely recognizes that this wasn't God's original intent for His creation. We feel the weight of the Fall when we grieve, a tiny taste of what Adam and Eve must have felt when the consequences of their sin involved that sudden removal from Eden and their separation from God's intimate presence. Loss is a transition that feels forced upon us, often takes us by surprise, and can easily make us feel overwhelmed and out of control (as if we were the ones running the universe in the first place!). The bottom line is: Letting go can be really, really hard, and none of us know what it will be like to walk through something we haven't yet experienced. That can feel a little unsettling and disorienting. It's vital for us in those times to know that there is Someone who will be there with us without fail, offering healing and comfort every step of the way.

Because of Jesus, we have an eternal hope that carries us through times of loss. Will it be easy? Of course not. But can we draw close to Him and make it through in one piece? Absolutely. Whether it's something that seems insignificant to the world (though not to us) or it's one of the most devastating situations we've ever faced, He is present. In fact, the Bible reminds us that God draws near to us in a special way during the toughest times: "The LORD is near to the brokenhearted" (Psalm 34:18 NASB). The comforting hymn "Be Still, My Soul" speaks to the heart about His presence with us no matter what we face:

> Be still, my soul: the Lord is on thy side.
> Bear patiently the cross of grief or pain;
> Leave to thy God to order and provide.
> In every change He faithful will remain.

As we've all learned, loss is an unavoidable part of our journey on this earth. But letting go is a different experience when we remember the One we're holding on to, who is forever holding on to us. He's not here merely for today; we get to wake up to Him tomorrow and every day after that until we see His face in glory. Then saying goodbye to anything or anyone will be a distant memory.

Dear Jesus, You are the One who never leaves my side.
Especially during the tough times,
I need to remember how close You are.
As I let go of so much in my life,
I want to always remember to hold on to You.
You are my one constant, and I am eternally grateful
for Your loving, faithful presence.

AMEN.

FOLLOW ON

YOU MAKE KNOWN TO ME THE PATH OF LIFE;
YOU WILL FILL ME WITH JOY IN YOUR PRESENCE.
PSALM 16:11 NIV

There's a lot of meaning packed into the word *adventure*. Just the sound of it inspires some of us to dream of undiscovered places, yet-to-be-attempted challenges, or memory-making road trips. But if we're honest, a lot of us seek those things less and less as we get older. Our world gets smaller and we get comfortable and decide it's not worth the risk (or the money or the energy) to make adventures happen. Of course, there are always people who are exceptions to the rule—like friends on social media who seem to pop up every other day with a photo of themselves in a new location or when they're trying something we've never even heard of. Sometimes we think, *Good for them!* Other times we think, *Wonder if I could do that someday* . . . Here's something to consider: adventure—as any good gift—can be a wonderful blessing from our Creator. Of course, that doesn't mean He intends for us to do everything all the time. But He *does* know precisely what lights us up, and He surely delights in seeing us experience the joy and wonder of something new when we feel the nudge to go for it. Plus, we all know that stepping out of our comfort zone even a little makes us less self-reliant and even more likely to reach out to Him.

Whether it's something as big as overcoming a fear of the unknown or as simple as learning to ask for what we need, anytime we recognize our limits is a chance for Him to "show up" for us in the way only He can. The most important thing about any opportunity is that we choose to walk closely with Him. It's not so much about what we're up to or where we're headed; it's about who we invite to come along. And when we allow Him to lead, we find unexpected joys along the way and experience a sense of peace and assurance that we never would have felt otherwise. The words to the hymn "Follow On" echo that truth. No matter where life leads us, we need only stick close to our Guide:

Down in the valley or upon the mountain steep,
Close beside my Savior would my soul ever keep;
He will lead me safely in the path that He has trod,
Up to where they gather on the hills of God.

Remember, trying new things doesn't have to mean skydiving, inventing something extraordinary, or sailing around the world. Even starting a challenging hobby, trying a new walking trail, or taking a day trip can be enough to jar us out of our comfort zone. If we ask Him—and keep our eyes and heart open—there's no telling what adventures He may have in store.

Lord, no matter what I do in my life,
I want to experience You in it.
When I'm inspired to go on adventures,
I want them to be with You, because Your presence
changes everything. I would never want to live without it.
As I open my eyes each day, remind me that You are the reason
I'm here and You are the One who leads every step of the way.
Thank You for being my constant companion on the journey.

AMEN.

FELLOWSHIP

SERVE ONE ANOTHER HUMBLY IN LOVE.
GALATIANS 5:13 NIV

Here's a thought to consider: Every day, someone you encounter is doing their best to adjust to something. It may be a small change—a new healthy habit, a different work or family schedule—or it might be something much bigger like moving to a new town or grieving the loss of a loved one. Whatever we are facing, we can all count on this: Life keeps moving, things keep changing, and none of us are able to stand still in the midst of it. But we always have the opportunity to help one another through those times as companions on the journey. Though here's the tricky thing: Often we don't even know *who* is going through *what*! That girl serving your coffee may be dealing with a bad breakup. It might be that teacher's first day on the job. The person on the phone may have been short with you because he'd just received some bad news from his doctor. Even our family members and close friends may keep things to themselves, struggling privately, when they could benefit so much from our support and encouragement. We all know how it feels because we've been there: When much of our energy is being used to deal with the changes we're facing, there may not be a lot left to help us function well in the day-to-day. We don't have much margin—our patience may be thin, we might be close to tears, or we're just being hard on ourselves about not meeting our own expectations.

Want to know who needs extra grace today? Ask God. Whether we're out and about, home in prayer, or somewhere in between, it only takes a moment to ask our loving Father how we might help someone through the challenges of today. And, remember, we may never know in this life how He answered that prayer. We might unknowingly arrive somewhere at just the right time or offer a much-needed smile, word of encouragement, or gift of grace. We may never hear a word from the other person about what they were going through or how we helped in that divinely appointed moment. But someday, as God's Word promises, all that is hidden will be made known. We will have the gift of seeing all the ways the Lord was able to use us to bring His kingdom to earth and His people to Himself. As the hymn "Fellowship" celebrates:

Sweet fellowship unites our souls as one;
It is the bliss of heaven now begun.
When heart to heart by this blest tie is bound,
We seem to stand each day on holy ground.

What a beautiful thought it is that we stand on holy ground when we serve each other in Him. The most ordinary day is made sacred as we offer ourselves as vessels for His love. The more we open our heart to the world around us and the Spirit within us, the more opportunities we'll have to bless and encourage those who need it most.

God, who needs extra grace today?
Who is dealing with change,
and how can I be a vessel for Your love?
Open my eyes and heart to the people around me.
Help me to be sensitive to Your Spirit within me.
Wherever I go, I want to be Your hands and feet in the world.
May I be a part of bringing Your kingdom to earth every day.

AMEN.

BE THOU MY VISION

AND WHATEVER YOU DO, IN WORD OR DEED,
DO EVERYTHING IN THE NAME OF THE LORD JESUS,
GIVING THANKS TO GOD THE FATHER THROUGH HIM.
COLOSSIANS 3:17 ESV

Whether we have one career in our lifetime or many different jobs along the way, the work we do will likely make up a big part of our days. We may meet some of our favorite people, learn some important things, deal with some conflict, hopefully enjoy some success, and probably experience a good bit of personal growth while we're working. Want to know what one of the biggest (and most daunting) growth experiences can be? A job change. Regardless of whether it's a change we wanted, it can be a stressful move—letting go of all that's familiar and maybe saying goodbye to a team we've been part of, while realizing that our current knowledge may not be so helpful in our new gig.

It's a good time to remind ourselves, then, of two important things. One: no matter what we're encountering, we're called to keep God first in our heart. He knows that those "in between" times can be especially disorienting. We've left behind what we knew, and we haven't yet found sure footing in what's ahead. The more we fix our eyes on Him, the more assurance we'll have in the transition. And two: We can remember that whatever we do, we are ultimately working for Him, not for people. No matter how challenging it might be to learn and adjust or how intimidated we may feel as we try to fit in, there's really no one we have to impress. All God asks is that we commit to doing honest work the best way we know how. We can honor those in authority and do our best to work well with our peers, but we have nothing to prove to anyone else as long as our eyes are on Him. It's quite freeing when we show up in a new situation without bringing unrealistic expectations of ourselves or the nagging fear that we may not measure up. The words of the hymn "Be Thou My Vision" are timeless, reminding us of how fulfilling it can be to live for Him alone:

> *Riches I heed not, nor man's empty praise;*
> *Thou mine inheritance, now and always;*
> *Thou and Thou only, first in my heart,*
> *High King of heaven, my treasure Thou art.*

The truth is, even if we've been working in one place for a while, none of us can know what tomorrow will bring. And even if it's not *us* going through the changes at the present time, there are others around us who are facing them. We can be the ones to extend a warm welcome to a new face. We can give grace and offer encouragement as they try to adjust to an unfamiliar environment. In the end, as long as we remember who we're truly working for, we can always find purpose and satisfaction in it. We can trust that we're right where we're meant to be until He leads us on.

Lord, remind me daily that You're the One I truly work for.
Even during those times when I'm not feeling it,
help me to be grateful for my job and the people
You've given me to work with. I want to be prepared for change,
knowing that You have plans I can't yet see.
Whether I'm in transition or settled somewhere,
help me to take it day by day, finding reasons to be thankful,
supporting and encouraging those around me,
and doing my best to honor You.

AMEN.

JUST AS I AM

NOW TO HIM WHO IS ABLE TO DO IMMEASURABLY MORE
THAN ALL WE ASK OR IMAGINE, ACCORDING TO HIS
POWER THAT IS AT WORK WITHIN US, TO HIM BE GLORY
IN THE CHURCH AND IN CHRIST JESUS THROUGHOUT ALL
GENERATIONS, FOR EVER AND EVER! AMEN.
EPHESIANS 3:20-21 NIV

This isn't an environmental lesson; it's a soul reflection. But first . . . a thought about recycling. We've all been encouraged to "reduce, reuse, recycle" to keep things from ending up in the landfill. When we throw something into the colorful bin, we may not know what it will become next, but at least we know that it won't contribute to the garbage heap. As materials are recycled, often they lose some of their quality, for obvious reasons. You can only repeat the cycle so many times until things break down enough that they can't be used again. "Upcycling," on the other hand, is a less familiar term. To upcycle something is to reuse it in such a way that it becomes a product of higher quality. To be upcycled, it doesn't have to be sent anywhere to be broken down. Instead, creativity is used to find new ways to repurpose the item. Maybe we take a stack of old newspapers and fold them to create a biodegradable flowerpot. Or we turn an old ladder into a bookshelf. Upcycling requires some imagination and time, but once we see the finished product, it can be so worth the effort. There's a sense of accomplishment in knowing that we created a new thing out of something that no longer seemed to have purpose. We took what was broken, forgotten, faded, or worn and made it into something that could be used and appreciated again.

Of course, here's the spiritual lesson in this: God is our great Upcycler. He's always ready to do a new thing with our old stuff. Those mistakes we've made, the habits that just seem to keep coming around, the attitudes that weigh us down every day . . . whatever that "mental material" is that we are so tired of, our Creator has a vision for it. He's ready to take something that feels like a dead end and make a new beginning out of it. And here's the most important part: He invites us to come to Him just as we are. Whatever we carry—whatever frustrations, past mistakes, broken dreams, or seemingly impossible relationships—He calls us to bring them to Him. Surely the beloved hymn "Just as I Am" has resonated through the years with so many because we have all faced our own imperfections countless times. And we know that there is only One who can make something truly beautiful out of the mess:

Just as I am, Thou wilt receive,
Wilt welcome, pardon, cleanse, relieve;
Because Thy promise I believe—
O Lamb of God, I come, I come.

There's nothing we need to fix or change before coming to Him. Not. One. Thing. He invites us to bring it all to Him—without shame. That's when the true journey begins. He knows us inside and out, He sees who we are becoming, and He will repurpose those things in our lives that are dragging us down. Let's come to Him today and every day, trusting that what is to come is infinitely greater than what we've ever known.

Father, knowing that You love me just as I am
brings me great peace for today.
And knowing that You are always working
in me brings me great hope for tomorrow.
I offer You all that I am, with all my imperfections,
trusting that You will work everything together for my good.

AMEN.

I NEED THEE EVERY HOUR

NO TEMPTATION HAS OVERTAKEN YOU EXCEPT WHAT IS
COMMON TO MANKIND. AND GOD IS FAITHFUL;
HE WILL NOT LET YOU BE TEMPTED BEYOND WHAT YOU
CAN BEAR. BUT WHEN YOU ARE TEMPTED, HE WILL ALSO
PROVIDE A WAY OUT SO THAT YOU CAN ENDURE IT.
I CORINTHIANS 10:13 NIV

Oh, temptation. It's exhausting sometimes. It seems like the same thing is trying to get the same foothold in life from every imaginable angle. It often feels like one of those old cartoons where a character is doing everything possible to keep a little leak from becoming a tidal wave. One hole is filled, but a new one opens up. Realistically, we feel as if we're managing pretty well with our struggles some days, but other days feel so overwhelming that we just want to throw in the proverbial towel. When today has been extra tough, we don't even want to think about what tomorrow might bring. But it's good to remind ourselves that we're not built to live for tomorrow. God designed us to live for *this* day—to trust Him for this one day and to draw near to Him especially during those long hours when we feel like giving up.

One of the most powerful ways to face temptation is rather unexpected: It's simply to stop fighting it. That doesn't mean to give up and let it overtake us. It means to stop doing the same old thing in our own strength and instead turn to our Maker for a new way through—His way. And His way begins in this moment, with Him. We shift our focus from our problem to His presence; we stop striving and start resting; we slow down to hear the still, small voice calling us to a new way of perceiving an old pattern. He is always here, in every moment, with all we need for a fresh start. The hymn "I Need Thee Every Hour" reminds us that His presence is what we need to seek first. Everything else will follow:

> *I need Thee every hour—*
> *Stay Thou nearby;*
> *Temptations lose their power*
> *When Thou art nigh.*

Nothing will change if we keep trying to fight old battles the same way. If we want to stop fighting, then we need to draw close to Him and start listening. In those quiet moments, a different way of being will begin to grow. His peace will calm us, His love will fill us, and His assurance will bring us new strength to carry us through our days. The more aware of God's presence we become, the less power those temptations have in our lives. Sure, it takes time to develop the daily practice of becoming more aware of Him, especially when we feel ourselves getting swept up into old patterns. But the more we lean in, the more we'll realize what a difference it can make. Need a little reminder to shift your focus when things get tough? Consider choosing a short verse or a bit of His truth to speak to yourself when temptation looms large. Remember: there will always be Someone who's bigger than anything you're facing, and He will always be there to lead you through.

Lord, I know that drawing near to You is the most powerful thing we can do each day. The answer to every need I have is found in Your presence. It's so simple, but I can make it so complicated sometimes. When I'm faced with temptation and try to fight my own battles, I pray that You will give me a gentle reminder to shift my focus to You, to rest in You, and listen for Your voice in my heart.

AMEN.

BUILT ON THE ROCK

DO YOU NOT KNOW THAT YOUR BODY IS A TEMPLE OF THE
HOLY SPIRIT WITHIN YOU, WHOM YOU HAVE FROM GOD?
YOU ARE NOT YOUR OWN, FOR YOU WERE BOUGHT
WITH A PRICE. SO GLORIFY GOD IN YOUR BODY.
I CORINTHIANS 6:19-20 ESV

It's mind-blowing to think that the God of the universe can choose any place to dwell, and yet He chooses to dwell in us. Not our buildings or our holy places (as wonderful as they are); not far away from us in an untouchable kingdom or hidden away from our human imperfection . . . just *right here, right now, within us.* What does that mean to us? Well, a lot of things, but one of the reasons is surely that these bodies we live in are sacred, and so is the body we belong to as believers in Christ. The hymn "Built on the Rock" celebrates the beautiful truth that we are "living stones" being built together. How we care for ourselves affects not only us but that greater body we've become part of:

> *We are God's house of living stones,*
> *Built for His own habitation;*
> *He fills our hearts, His humble thrones,*
> *Granting us life and salvation.*

Sometimes we do okay with self-care, finding some balance and giving ourselves what we need to progress. Other times—and this often happens during times of change in our lives—we become so focused on accomplishing things, proving ourselves, or covering so many bases that we begin running on empty before we realize it. Many of us have received this advice at some point, whether or not we wanted to hear it: "You need to take better care of yourself." We might have thought, *Really? And how might I do that? As if I need one more thing to add to my to-do list.* (Which probably proves the point!) Or it might be, *You're right. I've been aware of that, but I don't even know where to start.* Or perhaps, *I'm so done feeling this way. I'm tapped out. Just tell me what to do (or stop doing!) and I'm in.* We all have different levels of self-awareness, we all reach our breaking point in different ways, and we all have different reactions when we do reach our limit. But this is certain for every one of us: *we are human, God is God, and our quality of life depends largely on our remembering that.* We may feel as if we are superheroes after that giant cup of morning coffee . . . or when people praise us for saving the day by being everywhere at once . . . or when we somehow make it to the gym at 5:00 a.m. after three hours of sleep, but it just *can't* last. We are designed to live in a rhythm—to have times of refilling and renewal amid the constant movement of our lives.

God's Word points us toward taking a Sabbath rest, whatever that looks like for us. Jesus reminded the Pharisees that it's not about keeping another rule; it's about what we were designed to need: "The Sabbath was made for man, not man for the Sabbath" (Mark 2:27 NIV). That was probably a tough pill to swallow, since the Pharisees took such great pride in their self-sufficiency. And that can happen to us too. But burnout is a real thing, and when it happens, we need to remind ourselves of who dwells within is—the One who is always willing to bring us back into balance. Our job is merely to surrender.

Father, I long to sit in the quiet with You and listen.
What do I truly need right now? Is it more sleep?
Is it less technology? Do I need to make healthier choices?
Help me take care of myself. I want to be the best version
of myself so it will bring honor to Your name and
bring a little more goodness to Your kingdom on earth.

AMEN

GOD MOVES IN A MYSTERIOUS WAY

*"MY THOUGHTS ARE NOTHING LIKE YOUR THOUGHTS,"
SAYS THE LORD. "AND MY WAYS ARE FAR BEYOND
ANYTHING YOU COULD IMAGINE."*
ISAIAH 55:8 NLT

Perfectionism. Most of us have seen glimpses of it in ourselves or others—that need for flawlessness in some area . . . and that sense of disappointment, self-loathing, or frustration when it is not achieved. If you've ever struggled with perfectionism, you know how it can be like a troll following you around. It steals your time. Kills your imagination. Makes you not even want to *try* something new. When we think about it, that could be a solid tactic for the enemy of our souls. Nudging us to obsess about something that's unrealistic or unattainable at this moment in our lives and convincing us to exhaust ourselves in trying to make it happen anyway. That's some powerful ammunition. Our hyperfocus on any one thing can draw our attention away from everything else. We start striving for success under our own strength and lose sight of all the other joys of the journey.

Of course, it's wonderful to work hard and accomplish something we're passionate about! God gives us those ideas and dreams, and He surely delights in watching them come to life for us. But He also desires to be part of it all, drawing us closer to Him through everything we do. When we become too focused on our idea of perfection, we forget about His. And as we have learned from His Word, His ways are not our ways. Perhaps sometimes it's more about the process than the product. Maybe He's teaching us about new ways of seeing and being—and sometimes that can only happen through the experience of what feels like "failure" to us. The hymn "God Moves in a Mysterious Way" is all about trusting that process:

His purposes will ripen fast,
Unfolding every hour.
The bud may have a bitter taste,
But sweet will be the flower.

Bob Ross was an American artist who hosted *The Joy of Painting*, a well-known television show in the '80s where he painted live while instructing and offering words of encouragement to viewers. He was known for inspiring others to create fearlessly, without concern about messing up in the process. One of his most famous quotes, "We don't make mistakes, just happy little accidents," reflects his outlook: he saw the potential for something new where others could have seen failure. What a wonderful illustration of how we can live when we put all our endeavors into the hands of our Maker. We can do our best to create something beautiful with life, moving forward without fear while knowing that we can't predict what will happen in the process. But we can trust that He's always up to something wonderful—even through those things we perceive as mistakes. We can step boldly into our callings, both the daily ones and the big-picture ones, and we can let go of our need to control and instead watch for the new things that will unfold in our lives when we do.

Lord, sometimes I forget that earthly perfection is an illusion.
Thank You for reminding me that You're always up to
something more beautiful than I can imagine.
Help me to lay down all my striving and rest in You.
May I be a vessel to bring Your goodness and truth
to the world around me in whatever way You call me to.

AMEN.

GOD MOVES IN A
MYSTERIOUS WAY

God moves in a mysterious way
His wonders to perform.
He plants His footsteps in the sea
And rides upon the storm.

You fearful saints, fresh courage take;
The clouds you so much dread
Are big with mercy and shall break
In blessings on your head.

His purposes will ripen fast,
Unfolding every hour.
The bud may have a bitter taste,
But sweet will be the flower.

Blind unbelief is sure to err
And scan His work in vain.
God is His own interpreter,
And He will make it plain.

THERE'S A WIDENESS IN GOD'S MERCY

*SEE, I AM DOING A NEW THING! NOW IT SPRINGS UP;
DO YOU NOT PERCEIVE IT? I AM MAKING A WAY
IN THE WILDERNESS AND STREAMS IN THE WASTELAND.
ISAIAH 43:19 NIV*

It's amazing how different our tastes or preferences can be at different ages, in different cultures, with different backgrounds and experiences. We've all heard of the parent of a teenager wondering how in the world their kid could listen to that music ("Sounds like a bunch of noise!"). Or someone who can't imagine eating something considered a delicacy on the other side of the globe ("What in the world is that?!"). There's the guy driving his car to work who marvels at the biker headed to the same office ("That commute must be exhausting!"). Or the public-school mom observing the homeschool mom ("Who has the patience for that?"). Our differences keep life interesting, but they can also keep us from understanding each other. They can be an opportunity for growing apart—or, if we're open to it, our differences can inspire us to grow in new ways together. Observing others can motivate us to consider new perspectives or try new things. Many of us would admit that we find comfort in the familiar, and as we age, we may cling to our preferences more tightly, with little desire to consider other options. We may be less likely to think outside the box, let alone step into unfamiliar territory. But when we consider the endless possibilities in this marvelous universe we inhabit, we realize how much we miss when we refuse to leave our bubble. God knows that sometimes a new experience is just what we need, especially when we seem to be stuck in a rut. Being open to possibility can feed the spirit. Not only does it grow us, but it also helps connect us more deeply to our fellow humans—to consider their perspectives, to understand what brings them joy, and maybe even to learn to love something that we can do together.

Here's the greatest thing about broadening our horizons: the more we learn about and experience in this life, the more of our Creator we come to know. As His Word reminds us, "Everything comes from Him and exists by His power and is intended for His glory" (Romans 11:36 NLT). Those new opportunities to find joy and connection are His good gifts to us. His goodness is boundless, and His desire to bless us never wanes. The hymn "There's a Wideness in God's Mercy" illustrates that limitless love for us:

> *For the love of God is broader*
> *Than the measure of man's mind;*
> *And the heart of the Eternal*
> *Is most wonderfully kind.*

Of course, God is willing and able to bless us no matter what size of a life we live. Some of us will not venture very far out of our bubble during our lifetime, and while we will miss out on some wonderful experiences and connections, He loves us just the same. But for those who feel His nudge toward something different or "bigger" in our lives today, why not give it a try? Whether it's a little decision or a larger endeavor, we can trust that He is with us, delighting in our daily discoveries.

Heavenly Father, I want to keep my mind and heart open to possibility. Help me to be aware of the opportunities You provide me to try new things and understand others in fresh ways. This universe You've created is marvelous and filled with so much wonder! May I see and experience You everywhere.

AMEN.

TAKE TIME TO BE HOLY

BE COMPLETELY HUMBLE AND GENTLE;
BE PATIENT, BEARING WITH ONE ANOTHER IN LOVE.
EPHESIANS 4:2 NIV

Most of us have a preferred driving or walking route—a certain way we're so used to going that we end up on autopilot. Think of that early-morning exerciser who follows her trusted path through the neighborhood each day . . . the commuter who knows exactly where and when to avoid heavy traffic . . . the mom who finds the quickest way to the grocery store and sticks with it. It makes sense. Who has time for inefficiency these days? Of *course* we should do everything we can to avoid unnecessary obstacles . . . right? Many of us live with this mindset: *look for the easiest route; it's always the best one.* But there's another kind of "route" we take daily that has nothing to do with roads. It has to do with our relationships—those people we "do life with" every day.

Think about how often we prefer the "easy" way when it comes to interacting with our coworkers, friends, and loved ones. Once we get into a groove in any relationship, our connections can begin to feel so familiar that we find ourselves on autopilot. So when we encounter an obstacle, we quickly try to find our way around it. We might think, "I don't have time for this!" or "Why can't she just get over herself already?" or even, "What can I say that he wants to hear so that we can just move on?" Instead of trying to rush past those rough patches, God's Word invites us to see them in a new light. What we consider obstacles may very well be opportunities to grow closer (Proverbs 27:6). What we see as frustrating behavior in someone might be a mirror for us to look at ourselves (Matthew 7:3). What appears to be the easy path may lead us where we don't actually want to go (Matthew 7:14). This is certain when we face the choice between covering things up or digging deep with one another: Jesus would have us dig deep. He reminds us again and again that what's going on in our depths is infinitely more important that what's happening on the surface. He invites us to see our bumps in the road as opportunities for growth. And that means making our relationships a priority, because it takes time to learn to love one another well. We've heard it said that time is the new currency. When we take time for something, we are showing how valuable it is to us. The hymn "Take Time to Be Holy" reminds us to slow down and bring everything to Jesus:

Take time to be holy,
Be calm in thy soul,
Each thought and each motive
Beneath His control.

Jesus always took time for people. He never dismissed them; He never took the easy route or avoided the hard questions. He made the effort to see more deeply than their outer behavior . . . and we can do the same. Think of those "magic eye" pictures that we have to stare at for a while before the image emerges. Relationships can be like that too, when we give them the chance to develop. What appears is so worth the wait, but our job is to be present with each other long enough to allow it to happen.

Lord, help me to continually prioritize my relationships.
Help me learn to love others deeply.
When conflicts and challenges happen,
remind me that I don't have to run from them.
I want to use those times to discover the depth
of my connections and strengthen them with Your help.

AMEN.

IT IS WELL WITH MY SOUL

I AM LEAVING YOU WITH A GIFT—
PEACE OF MIND AND HEART.
AND THE PEACE I GIVE IS
A GIFT THE WORLD CANNOT GIVE.
SO DON'T BE TROUBLED OR AFRAID.
JOHN 14:27 NLT

It seems as if our natural human tendency in times of change and uncertainty is to find something (or someone) to hold on to. Think of a ship being tossed around in a stormy sea with everyone grasping for the closest thing to hold on to, determined to save themselves from those crashing waves! Whether there are big global shifts happening or more personal changes that are rearranging daily life, the ground beneath us can sometimes feel a little (or a lot!) shaky. And when that happens, we may begin to clutch for all kinds of things. Some of us reach for a sense of control—we try to control other things and even people to help reduce that feeling of chaos. Others dig up old habits and addictions, telling ourselves that we just need this or the other thing to get us through. Some people seek the latest book or movement that promises to help us rise above difficulty if we just follow certain steps. Regardless, here's something that often proves true in tough times: *we will most likely grasp whatever is closest to us at that moment of need.* So it makes sense that a little preparation can be helpful *before* the storm hits. Seasons of smooth sailing are excellent times to make that happen. Does it mean building a decent stash of healthy snacks to avoid a stressful chocolate binge? Or putting a few sticky notes on the mirror that remind us to release our white-knuckled need for control and "let go"? Sure, those ideas can be part of it! But the single greatest thing we can do to prepare for tomorrow's turbulence is to draw close to Christ today. God's Word reminds us that "He Himself is our peace" (Ephesians 2:14 NKJV). He's not telling us how to find peace, and He's not waiting for us to center ourselves so we'll finally receive it; He's offering us Himself in this moment, in smooth or rough water, whether we're feelin' it or not: "Peace be with you," He says to the fearful, confused disciples in the Upper Room. And He says it to us today. The hymn "It Is Well with My Soul" has comforted His followers ever since it was penned by someone who knew what it felt like to be tossed around with life's stormy sea:

> *When peace like a river attendeth my way,*
> *When sorrows like sea billows roll,*
> *Whatever my lot, Thou hast taught me to say,*
> *"It is well, it is well with my soul."*

We all make our own way through this life. Our loving Creator has given us that freedom, and we can navigate it however we choose. But let us never forget that drawing near to Him is always available to us at any moment. We may develop some positive practices and healthy habits to help us along the way, and it's important to learn ways that we can care for ourselves in mind, body, and soul. But through it all, let us remember the One who accompanies us, upholds us, and gives us His peace whenever and wherever we choose to turn to Him.

Jesus, I receive Your peace today. You are my Protector
and Sustainer through all the smooth and the rough times.
When I find myself reaching for something to steady me,
may I first reach for You—Your presence, Your Word,
and all the promises You have given me to stand on.
You are all I will ever need.

AMEN.

JESUS, I COME

I KNOW WHAT I'M DOING. I HAVE IT ALL PLANNED OUT—
PLANS TO TAKE CARE OF YOU, NOT ABANDON YOU,
PLANS TO GIVE YOU THE FUTURE YOU HOPE FOR.
JEREMIAH 29:11 THE MESSAGE

Children under eighteen years old make up roughly one-quarter of the world's population. So even if you aren't parenting one, you're likely to have a connection with a few! As we watch their lives unfold, those little ones can be mirrors for us—reminding us of our own early days, how carefree we were, how we may have struggled, and what we did to make sense of our lives and make our way to the adulthood we now inhabit. "Adulting" is a popular term these days, printed on T-shirts and coffee mugs, as people chuckle about the increased responsibility we carry as grown-ups and long for those endless days of childhood. But if we're honest with ourselves, it wasn't all roses. While some of us really did grow up within an idyllic family, others carry with them stories of dysfunction and disappointment. We all grew up in human families, though, and that means that nothing was perfect.

Whether we struggled a little or a lot, it can be hard to go back to the tough times in our mind and heart and admit the hurtful things that linger from the past. But sometimes that's just the step we need to take in order to free ourselves to move forward in life. As most of us have experienced, new beginnings often require endings of some sort, and letting go of old beliefs or behaviors can be tough; even if that's a grown-up we see in the mirror today, she (or he) is very much connected to the child we once were. But because of Jesus, we don't have to be afraid to ask the question, "What do I need to let go of in my life right now?" His promise to be with us is not simply for who we are now, but also for who we've always been and who we are becoming. He who exists outside of time knows exactly how you grew into your current self and exactly who you're growing into. There's a reason God calls us His children. We'll never outgrow our need for Him!

As we look at the little ones around us—marveling at their sense of wonder, cherishing their innocence, and longing to protect them in their vulnerability—let's remember that we were once in their shoes. Let's have grace for ourselves and all our ages. Let's remember that we, too, are children of a Father whose presence has never left us and never will. As the hymn "Jesus, I Come" reminds us, we can rest in His love and protection all the days of our lives.

Out of my bondage, sorrow and night,
Jesus, I come, Jesus, I come;
Into thy freedom, gladness, and light,
Jesus, I come to thee.

We are just as close to His heart as we've ever been. Like those little ones we cherish, we can rest in Him without worrying about tomorrow. We can trust that our past, present, and future are completely covered by His grace and blessed with His peace. All is well, because He lives.

Lord, what are the hurts and limitations
from my past that You want to free me of today?
How are You calling me to let go?
Thank You for holding my past, present,
and future in Your hands.
I know that all I need can be found in You.

AMEN.

I WANT JESUS TO WALK WITH ME

BUT WE ALL, WITH UNVEILED FACES,
LOOKING AS IN A MIRROR AT THE GLORY OF THE LORD,
ARE BEING TRANSFORMED INTO THE SAME IMAGE FROM
GLORY TO GLORY, JUST AS FROM THE LORD, THE SPIRIT.
II CORINTHIANS 3:18 NASB

Transformation is one of those wonderful words that motivates and inspires us. It may conjure up images of lowly caterpillars morphing into majestic butterflies, tiny seeds sprouting into vibrant flowers, or even one of those home makeover shows that turns a drab little room into a seemingly impossible masterpiece. There's something in us that responds to transformation, especially seeing the kind of beauty that can come from an unlikely place. Our heart is lifted when we witness a comeback or an unexpected change for the better. The transformation brings us a sense of hope and gives us new vision for our own less-than-stellar attempts and discouraging moments. We recognize that if something so "meh" can become something magnificent for someone else, then we have a shot, too, be it our beloved creation, our God-sized dream, or maybe that time in life when no one seems to understand the vision we have for something. These are all times when we need to remember the truth of that often-quoted but sometimes hard-to-believe verse, "With God all things are possible" (Matthew 19:26). As Jesus reminded His followers (and reminds us today!), even the tiniest seed can produce something we never thought possible.

Here's what we forget sometimes, though: pretty much every example of transformation will have some ugly parts in the middle. There will be some difficulty, some necessary "tearing down" in order to build up, some downright discouraging points between A and B when we wonder how we'll possibly make it, and doubt about whether we're even headed in the right direction! Think about it: A caterpillar's body has to completely break down before those wings emerge. A seed sits in the dark for a long time before things start happening. And before that little shack becomes a jaw-dropping mansion, there is a *lot* of dust and dismantling involved. Why is it important to remember these things? Because we need to be ready for them. Change is inevitable . . . but allowing ourselves to be truly *transformed* by it is our decision. Whatever happens can always be used for our good and God's glory, if we're open to it. And our Jesus is the One who stands ready to lead us through. The song "I Want Jesus to Walk With Me" comforts us as we reach out to God with all our wants and cares:

I want Jesus to walk with me.
I want Jesus to walk with me.
All along my pilgrim journey,
Lord, I want Jesus to walk with me.

We serve a marvelous Creator who desires our continual transformation from glory to glory as we are being made in the image of His Son. Jesus knows what it is like to walk this world in our humanity. May we never forget that He is always with us on the path between where we were and where we're headed. He is not only the catalyst for our transformation, but He also offers His presence in the process and for all eternity. Let's rest in that as we become all He has created us to be.

Jesus, You're the One who brings beauty from ashes,
hope from despair, light in darkness, life from death.
I praise You for being my constant Companion on this journey
and transforming my life in ways I never imagined.
Remind me of that beautiful truth when I forget the big picture.
Your presence is all I need to see me through.

AMEN.

I SURRENDER ALL

*BUT FEW THINGS ARE NEEDED—
OR INDEED ONLY ONE.
MARY HAS CHOSEN WHAT IS BETTER,
AND IT WILL NOT BE TAKEN AWAY FROM HER.*
LUKE 10:42 NIV

We hear the word *simplify* a lot these days, and it means different things at different times for each of us. It may be a massive decluttering effort in our home when we realize we have more stuff than space, weeding out some calendar commitments when we've given away all our time, paring down our diets when we discover we have too much "fake" and not enough "fresh," or even minimizing our circle of friends. (The older we get, the more we realize how precious our time is and generally become more intentional about who we're spending it with!) But isn't it funny how strange it can feel to simplify? Living in a consumer culture can keep us on a kind of default setting that convinces us we need more, more, and more. And not just with material things, but with people, experiences, achievements . . . the list can go on. It's as if our worth goes up with every new something (or someone) we acquire in life. We buy and build, connect and create—and there's nothing wrong with those things! They can be wonderful, God-given opportunities for us. But when our lives start to fill up with more stuff than Spirit, we may sense the loving nudge of our heavenly Father as He calls us to slow down and make a change. Is He against us having nice things? Or lots of friends? Or successful endeavors? We all know that answer—of course not. He loves to bless us and surely delights in our enjoyment of those good gifts. But He also knows how quickly we can become distracted, overwhelmed, and overrun by what we acquire when we don't keep it in check. We can compromise our connection with Him in the name of meeting people, going places, and getting things done. We may fall into bed at night and belatedly realize that the day was filled with everything but the awareness of His sweet presence. We all do it, and we all need a reminder now and then to slow down and open our minds, hearts, and hands to allow Him to remove what has come between us. Consider the words of the hymn "I Surrender All":

All to Jesus, I surrender,
All to Him I freely give;
I will ever love and trust Him,
In His presence daily live.

When it comes to simplifying, there's only one thing we're actually being asked to do as followers of Christ: *surrender.* Everything else flows from that. It will look different for each of us, but it will likely involve quieting ourselves in some way to listen for that still, small voice. As we prayerfully consider all the things, commitments, experiences, and relationships we've acquired, we can ask what it may be time to let go of in this season of life. As we learn more each day how to loosen our grip on everything else, we find more peace in Him. We can trust that when it's time to make a change, He will show us when and how.

Lord, thank You for Your countless blessings in this life.
All that I have is Yours, and I know I forget that sometimes.
I find myself holding too tightly to things,
especially those things You would have me let go of
for my own good. Help me to daily surrender it all to You,
to listen for Your guidance,
and to simply trust in Your life-giving love.

AMEN.

LOVE DIVINE, ALL LOVES EXCELLING

AND THE SEEDS THAT FELL ON THE GOOD SOIL
REPRESENT HONEST, GOOD-HEARTED PEOPLE
WHO HEAR GOD'S WORD, CLING TO IT,
AND PATIENTLY PRODUCE A HUGE HARVEST.
LUKE 8:15 NLT

Experienced gardeners know just how important it is to understand the details of their environment before planting anything. Climate, soil quality, the amount of sun or shade, protection from hungry critters . . . a lot of details come together to help ensure the health and growth of the seeds they scatter. When we see a thriving garden, it's easy to forget how much planning went into its fruition. It is a lovely illustration of the way our heavenly Father nurtures growth in us. He is wonderfully intentional. When He invites us to take new steps, we can be sure that He has already prepared our environment. Where we are today—our specific town, neighborhood, job, family, circumstances—they all matter for lots of reasons. God knows exactly where, when, and how our growth can happen, and He offers us every opportunity for transformation to take place.

But unlike the seeds in a physical garden, we have a choice about whether we will change. When we hear that still, small voice nudging us toward change, we can always choose to ignore it (and if we're honest, sometimes we do!) or we can argue with it—or we can surrender to it and be open to whatever new experience He's calling us into. When we choose the last option, things start to make more sense about our current situation. We realize that the details of our lives are never accidents. That "difficult" neighbor, an unexpected job opportunity, the idea someone shared that made a "light bulb" come on for us . . . every little part of our lives is lined up to prepare us for whatever is ahead. Every detail matters to Him and should matter to us too. His Word reminds us that all things are working together for the good of those who love Him, and sometimes "good" means "growth," which isn't always an easy process. That's why when it hurts (and sometimes it just does!), we need to remember that it's all leading somewhere—and not just *somewhere*, but to our ultimate wholeness in Him. "Love Divine, All Loves Excelling" is a hymn that reminds us of God's life-changing love that accompanies us on the journey:

Finish, then, Thy new creation;
Pure and spotless let us be.
Let us see Thy great salvation
Perfectly restored in Thee.

God's love is all we need to be transformed into the image of Jesus. His love is the reason that He allows our lives to unfold the way they do. Nothing is meaningless; everything can be used for our growth if we'll allow it. When we know that our days are in His hands, we don't have to wonder where it's all headed. We can trust that He will provide whatever is most needed for our good and His glory.

Lord, "growing" hurts sometimes!
I don't like being uncomfortable,
even though I know that what You are doing in me
is so worth whatever I'm going through.
When I see something beautiful in Your creation,
I want to remember that. Thank You for giving us
glimpses of Your truth and love everywhere.
Help me to find comfort and strength in Your presence
in every season of my life.

AMEN.

TAKE MY LIFE AND LET IT BE

YOU SHOW THAT YOU ARE A LETTER FROM CHRIST,
THE RESULT OF OUR MINISTRY,
WRITTEN NOT WITH INK BUT WITH THE SPIRIT
OF THE LIVING GOD, NOT ON TABLETS OF STONE
BUT ON TABLETS OF HUMAN HEARTS.
II CORINTHIANS 3:3 NIV

We are all unique, so letting God lead us will look different for each of us at any point along the journey. But one thing we can all do in His Name, anytime, is to support one another in what we're going through. The hymn "Take My Life and Let It Be" is a wonderful reminder of the joy that comes from putting our lives in His hands and offering ourselves as vessels for His love:

> Take my hands and let them move
> At the impulse of Thy love.
> Take my feet and let them be
> Swift and beautiful for Thee.

Some of the greatest opportunities to live out that love come when our brothers and sisters are going through times of change. It may be a spiritual shift—like feeling called to go deeper with God, shedding layers from their old lives, or beginning a new practice that helps them become more centered in Him. When we know that someone is taking significant spiritual steps, we can pause a moment to encourage them or talk about our own experiences and remind them that they're not alone. Share some inspiration with them or ask how we can be praying for them.

The change they're undergoing could be in the realm of relationships—the blessed beginning or difficult end of a marriage, working through family dynamics, or welcoming a child or becoming a caretaker for a loved one. We may sense their struggle to find balance or just assume, based on our own experience, that there will be an adjustment period. Sometimes that kind of change is very personal, and even if we don't address it directly, we can always make a point to connect with them regularly. We can check in just to see how life is going and offer our presence in case they need a listening ear or physical help. And lastly, here's a tough but important opportunity for support. We may know someone who realizes they *need* to make a change but feels afraid to move forward. Maybe they're worried about what others will think or even fear that they don't have the strength to see it through. There may be an unhealthy habit they want to quit, something at work they need to address, or a move toward a God-sized dream that requires courage.

Of course, we can't do things *for* our friends; it's their journey to take. They are the only ones who can step into what they are uniquely called to do. But we can offer them the presence of Christ in our own way. We can remember the times when we have been in their shoes and someone showed up for us in a way that was desperately needed. With God's Spirit living in us, we can be part of someone's answered prayer. What an honor to be His vessels, bringing His kingdom to life for one another.

Lord, I want to be a vessel for Your love.
I want to show up for those who need it most,
and I trust that You'll guide me toward them.
Help me to keep my heart and mind open,
to always be present with the compassion of Jesus.

AMEN.

O LOVE THAT WILT NOT LET ME GO

SO WE FIX OUR EYES NOT ON WHAT IS SEEN,
BUT ON WHAT IS UNSEEN,
SINCE WHAT IS SEEN IS TEMPORARY,
BUT WHAT IS UNSEEN IS ETERNAL.
II CORINTHIANS 4:18 NIV

Disappointment is one of those tough feelings for us humans, and no matter how hard we try to avoid it, at some point, in some way, we have to face it. And sometimes that can happen during a season of much-needed change in our lives. We may have come to what people refer to as a "tipping point," feeling as if something needs to shift but we're not sure what or how. We might be feeling extreme discomfort, facing a lack of resources, or realizing we need to get out of an unhealthy situation. So what do we do? We just make the changes we need and move on, right? It sounds simple enough. But what happens when it's not only in our hands—when there are circumstances or relationships involved that are beyond our control? That can be such a helpless feeling. We may begin to feel overwhelmed and even project our fears into the future, wondering what we will do if everything stays the same.

Before we allow the what-ifs to take over, there are a few things that we can remind ourselves. First: Even if things don't happen the way we're hoping they will, it's going to be okay. We may not be able to see what "okay" looks like at that moment, but we have to trust that, in God's hands, our lives will always work out for our best. Second: In those times when we feel fear or anxiety welling up, we can find a few quiet moments and become deeply aware of our Savior's presence. We can remember that He sees our lives from beginning to end. And while our hoped-for change may not be fulfilled in the way we think it should be, He will always make a better way for us. Most importantly, our ultimate hope will be realized in Him one day and disappointment will be a thing of the past forever. "O Love That Wilt Not Let Me Go" has been sung throughout the years to bring people that reminder of hope when they need it most:

> O Love that will not let me go,
> I rest my weary soul in Thee.
> I give Thee back the life I owe,
> That in Thine ocean depths its flow
> May richer, fuller be.

What wonderful sense of relief and assurance He has promised! We can draw close to Him, especially during uncertain times when we're not sure how it's all going to work out. The more we focus on His goodness and all the ways we see it around (and within!) us, the less we sink into despair and discouragement. The more we place our trust in Him, the less we depend on certain outcomes for our happiness and fulfillment. So let's do what we can, hope for the best, and remember that He's already provided what we need most—the gift of Himself—for every moment of our lives.

> *Lord Jesus, You are my hope forever.*
> *May I hold tightly to that truth each day,*
> *no matter what life brings.*
> *When I face those much-needed changes,*
> *I trust that You will guide me through them.*
> *Help me let go of my ideas of how things should be*
> *and open my heart to whatever You have for me.*
> *I could never ask for more than*
> *Your faithful, loving presence in my life.*

AMEN.

O LOVE THAT WILT NOT LET ME GO

O Love that will not let me go,
I rest my weary soul in Thee.
I give Thee back the life I owe,
That in Thine ocean depths its flow
May richer, fuller be.

O Light that follows all my way,
I yield my flick'ring torch to Thee.
My heart restores its borrowed ray,
That in Thy sunshine's blaze its day
May brighter, fairer be.

O Joy that seekest me through pain,
I cannot close my heart to Thee.
I trace the rainbow through the rain,
And feel the promise is not vain,
That morn shall tearless be.

O Cross that liftest up my head,
I dare not ask to fly from Thee.
I lay in dust, life's glory dead,
And from the ground there blossoms red,
Life that shall endless be.

WONDERFUL PEACE

Most of us know someone who seems to be a wanderer. Even in the earliest years of life, there's that kid in kindergarten who just can't stay in his or her chair for very long. Or the daughter who transfers colleges three times before earning her degree. Then there's the relative who seems to have a different job every time we see them or the friend who visits more places in a year than we've seen in our lifetime. Regardless, you get the picture. There's not a lot of staying in one place for these folks. Opportunities for new experiences, environments, and explorations rise to the top of their list, and the thought of being stuck somewhere forever may feel like torture.

Sometimes this desire for newness is just part of our makeup—a God-given passion for seeing and savoring all He has created and provided in this great big world. The people, sights, sounds, experiences . . . all the details He's blessed us with to take in and enjoy—there's just something within many of us that is drawn to change, and that is a beautiful thing! Even if we aren't particularly adventurers, we all get the urge to go places, to do things, and to make changes in our lives. But when we find ourselves doing more than usual, we might want to check in and ask why.

Sometimes, as much as we hate to admit it, we seek out new opportunities because we don't want to see something in our current situation. When we feel restless on the inside, it can make us want to switch things up on the outside in order to avoid whatever it is within us that's asking for our attention. There may be an issue that needs to be addressed and we simply don't want to go there. When God's Spirit lives in us, we have His Counselor available anytime. When we take the time to sit quietly and prayerfully in His presence, He can help us explore our motives and our true needs. If we imagine our lives as a pendulum, we can remember, when we sense we're swinging too far, that His Spirit is our quiet center. He is the place we can always come home to before making all those plans and changes. We can return to Him, rest in Him, and listen for His voice of guidance, as the soothing hymn "Wonderful Peace" reminds us:

What a treasure I have in this wonderful peace,
Buried deep in the heart of my soul,
So secure that no power can mine it away
While the years of eternity roll!

Jesus showed us that it's not about what we're doing on the outside; it's always about what's happening within. That's what He cares about, because that's the eternal part of us. So if you're truly ready for a change, that's wonderful! Just remember, He is there to help you decide whether it's the right thing for you at this time. If it is, go for it! And if it isn't, you can ask Him to "shine a light" on anything you may need to see within yourself first. You can trust that, in time, He will make it clear when you're truly ready to step into something new.

Heavenly Father, thank You for the countless adventures
and experiences You bless us with in this life.
May I always be open to the wonderful opportunities
You have for me. Help me to be sensitive to the voice of
Your Spirit so that I can determine my true motivations.
No matter what I do, I want to live freely
and joyfully in Christ.

AMEN.

ALL THE WAY, MY SAVIOR LEADS ME

SLOW DOWN. TAKE A DEEP BREATH. WHAT'S THE HURRY?
WHY WEAR YOURSELF OUT?
JUST WHAT ARE YOU AFTER ANYWAY?
JEREMIAH 2:25 THE MESSAGE

Think about the messages you've heard throughout your life about achievement, accomplishment, and success. They're different for each of us; depending on our culture and upbringing, we all absorbed our own understandings about what a fruitful and purposeful life looks like. No matter what we've been taught to aim for, there is often a sense of urgency about reaching those goals: Get good grades and get a good job. Make things happen and make a big difference. Many of us have been routinely encouraged (even in ministry!) to do more, be more, and have more to show for it. Especially in these times, the world around us seems to say, "Hurry! There's so much to do and so little time!" That's why, when we sense the Spirit's call to slow down a bit, it can feel very strange. Being asked to downshift can feel like this scenario: Imagine a marathon runner who is having some great momentum, but all of a sudden, she's nudged out of the race. It makes no sense. None of the other runners are dragging their feet. There's a finish line up ahead, and she has her eye on the prize!

Of course, our heavenly Father knows exactly what we're attempting during our seasons of life, along with why He's calling us to change things up. He sees our deepest motives. He knows what's driving us to rush and why we may be feeling the need to prove ourselves. And he's also aware of what we may be sacrificing in order to do that. When He calls us to slow down, it's not always because we're headed in the wrong direction; it's just that we may be missing some important details along the way—people to connect with, blessings to discover, joys to share, wisdom to receive, or more. He knows it's not about those earthly destinations for which we may find ourselves striving; it's about all the steps we take in the process that bring us closer to Him and to one another. "All the Way, My Savior Leads Me" is a hymn that reminds us of His constant guidance on the journey, providing just what we need when we need it.

All the way my Savior leads me;
What have I to ask beside?
Can I doubt His tender mercy,
Who through life has been my Guide?

When we think of Jesus moving through His life on earth, most of us envision the slower pace of that ancient time. There weren't many faster options to choose from back then! Traveling, gathering for prayer, preparing and sharing a meal . . . things were simpler— and most likely savored in a deeper way because they could not be rushed. Let's remember that when we sense the nudge to stop, to be more present on the journey and less driven toward the goal. We'll get wherever He's leading us in His time. All we have to do is keep our heart open to His leading along the way.

Lord, slowing down can feel so strange
in this fast-moving world.
But when You're nudging me to downshift,
I don't ever want to miss it!
Even though I may have goals and destinations
set in my life, I know that You can see the bigger picture,
and I trust You to walk with me, to set the pace,
and to take me where You know I need to go.

AMEN.

MY SHEPHERD WILL SUPPLY MY NEED

THE LORD IS MY SHEPHERD; I HAVE ALL THAT I NEED.
HE LETS ME REST IN GREEN MEADOWS;
HE LEADS ME BESIDE PEACEFUL STREAMS.
PSALM 23:1–2 NLT

One of the most unsettling things about unexpected change is that we don't have time to plan for it. That's not so hard for the free spirits among us, but for those who aren't fond of spontaneity and who feel a little panicky when we're unprepared . . . it can be brutal! Whether it be the loss of a job, a sudden move, the end of an unhealthy relationship or an urgent transition for our families, we can feel like we're standing at a precipice, about to step off into the unknown. We may think things like: What if it doesn't work out? What if I don't have the strength? What if there's not enough money or time or help to make it happen?

While our wandering human minds are busy dredging up all kinds of fear, our omniscient Creator is doing just the opposite: He is expanding our capacity for faith, and He knows just how to make that happen. As much as we hate to admit it sometimes, our trust muscles are not built on the easy road. Our self-sufficiency shines in the business-as-usual times—when we have a pretty good idea of what will be happening tomorrow and have the resources to sustain us. Sure, we may have a healthy prayer life in times of smoother sailing, but our connection with Him can feel more like a nice support than a true necessity.

Our times of need will always ebb and flow, and that's okay. That's how it works in relationships—sometimes we're connected intensely, and other times, the bond feels different. Imagine a parent and child walking hand-in-hand. In some circumstances, that little one's grip is loose and carefree, enjoying the company of his or her guardian. Other times, they will hold on for dear life to be reassured that they are not alone. It all depends on what they're walking through. And what do they need more than anything in the fearful moments? To know their protector is present and will not let go. "My Shepherd Will Supply My Need" is a beautiful reminder of that for us. Based on the comforting words of Psalm 23, the hymn reassures us that there is a place for us to rest amidst our fears and uncertainties:

Here would I find a settled rest,
While others go and come;
No more a stranger, nor a guest,
But like a child at home.

No matter where we are headed or what we will face, our Shepherd has promised us His presence. What more could we need? There will be hard days and times of doubt and discomfort, but there will always be a haven that awaits us, anytime, anywhere, when we turn our hearts toward Him.

Lord, I know I can't predict the changes to come.
I wish I could sometimes, but I realize that's just not how this
life works. I know I can trust that You're always up to something
good, even when I can't see more than one step ahead on the
journey. Your presence is all I've ever needed, and You've shown
me in so many ways that You are always enough, no matter what
my doubts, fears or circumstances would lead me to believe.
Thank You for being my Provider, Protector, Comforter and
Helper. Thank You for being present with me, at any hour.
When I'm feeling afraid or uncertain about what life may bring,
help me to remember to turn my heart toward You.

AMEN.

BLEST BE THE TIE THAT BINDS

SO WE, THOUGH MANY, ARE ONE BODY IN CHRIST,
AND INDIVIDUALLY MEMBERS ONE OF ANOTHER.
ROMANS 12:5 ESV

The hymn "Blest Be the Tie That Binds" celebrates the path we walk together through this life, supporting each other in prayer, serving one another in love, and sharing our joys and burdens along the way. When we invest deeply in relationships with our brothers and sisters in Christ, we can experience a powerful connection that's truly not of this world. Sure, we are all human beings with quirks who are struggling to navigate relationships in our own ways, but the "tie" that binds us—our life in Christ—brings us a mutual understanding and capacity for the kind of love that just isn't possible from our own human strength. This is a beautiful thing, but it can also mean some big adjustments (and maybe more than a little sadness) when those connections have to change. If we had our way, we'd keep our favorite people close forever, but God sometimes has other plans. Maybe someone dear to us is moving away, transitioning out of a job or church community that brought us together. Or we might be feeling that complicated nudge to allow more space in a relationship. Whatever the circumstances, as we pull away, it can feel like trying to unstick superglue.

In Christ, we've become part of something much bigger than ourselves, and our lives are intertwined in more ways than we can see. We're not merely casual friends—we're part of a spiritual family! But the good news is, that fact doesn't have to change, no matter how far apart we are or how often we're able to connect. Yes, there will be sadness and maybe even frustration or disappointment in the separation. When someone we've felt a strong bond with can't be part of our lives in the same way, we'll need some time to adjust and find peace with it. But the connection can always be there, just as strong as ever. God's Word reminds us in many ways that what is unseen is more real and powerful than we can imagine. Not even death can come between us in the end. Think of that! Even when we have to say a final earthly goodbye, the tie that binds us does not loosen one bit. The same Christ who holds us in this life holds us in the next. In Him, "we live and move and have our being" . . . together (see Acts 17:28 ESV). As the hymn reminds us:

> When we are called to part,
> It gives us inward pain,
> But we shall still be joined in heart
> And hope to meet again.

So let's celebrate and savor our relationships with our brothers and sisters regardless of actual proximity. We can trust that our Father holds each of those connections in His hands. He knows why we have been brought close for a season (or a lifetime!), and He will provide all we need as we navigate the changes ahead. Whether we have the joy of connecting face-to-face, from a distance, or even through prayer, there is one body and one Spirit, and we belong to that beautiful family forever.

Father God, I love being part of Your ever-growing family.
Thank You for the wonderful connections
You've given me with my brothers and sisters in Christ.
In whatever way those relationships change through the years,
remind me often that You are the One
who connects us for all eternity.

AMEN.

LEAD US, HEAVENLY FATHER, LEAD US

HE STILLED THE STORM TO A WHISPER;
THE WAVES OF THE SEA WERE HUSHED.
PSALM 107:29 NIV

Have you ever sat on a beach and watched people interact with the ocean? Young children right at the edge squeal with delight while the water laps their toes. A surfer lays on a board farther out, waiting for the right moment to catch the perfect wave. Swimmers navigate currents, lifeguards observe intently, and divers search for that ideal spot to view underwater wonders. It's the same sea for each of these people—the same amount of water, the same windswept surges, and the same moments of calm that settle in now and then. The difference is in every person's perspective: What are they expecting? What are they afraid of? What are they hoping for? The way a person relates to the water will determine their experience of it. They'll have a sense of resistance, hypervigilance, adventure, or wonder . . . all depending on the way they perceive themselves and the water surrounding them. The surfer is preparing for the challenge; the child is finding joy in the moment; the lifeguard is protecting others; the diver is in discovery mode.

You may have figured out that the sea represents our lives. Just like life, it never stops moving. There are chaotic times that make us sense more than ever our lack of control . . . and that can be scary. And there are times that are calmer; we feel grateful and maybe even a little apprehensive because we know that nothing stays the same for long. The thing we need to remember in all those moments is the anchor that holds us, regardless of how many waves we face or how high they may be. There is One who created the sea of our lives and surrounds us with His presence in it every moment of every day. It's extra important to remind ourselves of that fact during times of transition. Those times are when we may feel the most overwhelmed and out of control. But we always have the choice about how we're going to navigate it all. That energy we're tempted to pour into fear and hesitation can be redirected toward trust and prayer. We can set aside time with our heavenly Father and find that calm center with Him in the midst of all that movement in our lives. We can find that peaceful place within us where His Spirit resides throughout the day. The hymn "Lead Us, Heavenly Father, Lead Us" reminds us that nothing can steal our peace when we choose to rest in Him:

Lead us, heavenly Father, lead us
O'er the world's tempestuous sea;
Guard us, guide us, keep us, feed us,
For we have no help but Thee.

As many of us have learned, life is not about quantity; it's about quality. The way we choose to see our lives will determine our experience, and as we look back, we'll see that our years have been filled with the choices we make every day. If we daily choose to invite the One who made us to guide us through, our lives will hold a richness and supernatural peace that no earthly source can provide.

Jesus, You are my peace.
No matter what circumstances life brings,
no matter how much I doubt or fear,
Your Spirit is present within me to calm the sea of my life.
I praise You for all You are, and I need Your help
to remember that Your love is my eternal anchor.
May I begin and end every day
with that soul-deep awareness.

AMEN.

FOR THE BEAUTY OF THE EARTH

FOR SINCE THE CREATION OF THE WORLD GOD'S
INVISIBLE QUALITIES—HIS ETERNAL POWER
AND DIVINE NATURE—HAVE BEEN CLEARLY SEEN,
BEING UNDERSTOOD FROM WHAT HAS BEEN MADE,
SO THAT PEOPLE ARE WITHOUT EXCUSE.
ROMANS 1:20 NIV

Many of us find a special connection with our Creator through His creation. As we experience the magnificence of our natural surroundings, from the towering majesty of an oak tree to the tiniest details of a wildflower, we can't help but marvel at the One who orchestrated it all. The Bible has a lot to say about how nature reflects His glory, reveals His heart for us, and reminds us that every living thing depends on Him to survive, grow, and flourish. One of the many ways the natural world can draw us closer to our Maker is by reflecting the way life works—all of life, not just plants and animals but our human and spiritual lives too. Our loving Father has made it clear that death and loss will never have the last word. He seems to have woven that truth into the world around us. Think of the elements, the constant presence of water on the earth . . . how it never truly ends but just changes form as it plays its part in sustaining our intricate ecosystem. Or consider the seasons . . . the leaves of autumn fading and falling, becoming part of the earth again and helping to nourish what will sprout in the spring. Even Jesus uses a natural explanation to illustrate the concept of resurrection in John 12:24: "Unless a seed falls to the ground and dies, it cannot bear fruit" (paraphrase).

It doesn't take a fancy degree to observe and understand the way nature works. As Romans 1:20 reminds us, it is one way God has chosen to reveal Himself that no one can deny. That's something we can remember when we encounter what feels like an ending in our lives. It may be the end of a particular season, a relationship, a job, or an endeavor we pursued for a while. It could be letting go of something we've been holding on to for a long time. It could be the unexpected close of a chapter in our lives that we thought we'd just begun to write. Whatever it is, we can trust that as hard as endings can be, there is always something new beginning even when we can't see it. Scripture reminds us that in Christ "all things have become new" (II Corinthians 5:17 NKJV). That's the pattern of the world: when something dies, new life is being created; when something is taken away, a new space is opening up. And as we observe this taking place around us, we can be sure that it happens within us too. As the hymn "For the Beauty of the Earth" reminds us, the love of God is visible in everything:

For the beauty of the earth,
For the glory of the skies,
For the love which from our birth
Over and around us lies.

Let's never stop marveling at Creation and the way it reveals the heart of our Maker for us. Just think—the One who creates, sustains, and transforms all of life lives within us by His Spirit. When we experience those endings in our lives, we can hold fast to His promises for greater things to come. Even as we let go, He is already orchestrating something beautiful and new.

Father, as I marvel at Your creation, I sense the love You pour out for all of us in so many unique ways. I see hope and renewal in the pattern of this world You have made, and I am grateful for every opportunity You give me to experience it in my life.

AMEN.

MY HOPE IS BUILT ON NOTHING LESS

THE RAIN CAME DOWN, THE STREAMS ROSE,
AND THE WINDS BLEW AND BEAT AGAINST THAT HOUSE;
YET IT DID NOT FALL,
BECAUSE IT HAD ITS FOUNDATION ON THE ROCK.
MATTHEW 7:25 NIV

Moving day: two words that will matter greatly to most of us at some point in our lives. For some, those words will bring a sense of excitement and adventure; for others, sadness and nostalgia; and for many . . . a little bit of everything. Moving is a big deal. It's listed as one of the five most stressful life events—and for good reason! Whether we're going across town or across the country, we're packing up our past, saying goodbye to what's familiar, and heading out in hopes of making a new life somewhere. New walls, new faces, new places to find our necessities, new routes, new rules, new pretty-much-everything . . . that's a lot of adjustment happening in a short amount of time. As with any change, this one can keep us feeling "up in the air" for a while. Plus, we may be starting a new job, helping kids acclimate, feeling extra emotional, dealing with new bills and paperwork, and so much more!

It's important during these times to be intentional about caring for ourselves—something we can easily forget in stressful situations. We can start by covering our move in prayer from the beginning, asking the Father to bless every detail and provide the help we'll need (physically, emotionally, and spiritually). We can set aside a little time each day to rest in His presence, even if it's just ten minutes in a quiet place away from the moving boxes and mayhem. If we don't have a church yet, we can still put out feelers to connect with other

Christ followers for some much-needed spiritual support. And lastly, we can remind ourselves often that no matter how many times we change houses and locations in this life, our true home will always be found in Him. As we build a life in a new place, let's remember the never-changing foundation that our life is already built on. The hymn "My Hope Is Built on Nothing Less" is a beautiful reminder of that truth:

> *My hope is built on nothing less*
> *Than Jesus's blood and righteousness;*
> *I dare not trust the sweetest frame,*
> *But wholly lean on Jesus's name.*

Even if we're not the ones packing up, we may know someone who is or will be. What a great opportunity to love on our brothers and sisters. They may not ask for help, but there's a 99 percent chance they need it! Let's be the ones who show up in whatever way we can to lighten the load during such a significant transition. Maybe we can offer to lend a hand with kids, fill out a few forms, box up some trinkets—an extra hand can make a big difference! No matter what part we play in a move, we can rest assured that the Lord will be with us all the way. It's a good reminder for us and for those who may be on the journey today.

Lord, no matter where I settle, You will always be my true home.
My life is built on the eternal foundation of Your love,
and my heart is Yours. I pray that You will bless and
protect all those who are moving today and that,
when it's my turn, I will trust You to care for every detail.
Thank You for all the wonderful ways You provide for us
and see us through the changes in our lives.

AMEN.

AMAZING GRACE

GRACE AND PEACE TO YOU MANY TIMES OVER
AS YOU DEEPEN IN YOUR EXPERIENCE WITH GOD
AND JESUS, OUR MASTER.
II PETER 1:2 THE MESSAGE

"Amazing Grace" is listed as one of the most beloved hymns of all time, and for good reason. It's a song of remembrance many of us can relate to through our journey of following Jesus. Coming to know Him is one of those transitions that never truly ends. God's Word reminds us that we "are being transformed into His image with ever-increasing glory" (II Corinthians 3:18 NIV). No matter how long it has been since our heart became His, there's a sweetness to recalling those first steps with Him. And it's not just about nostalgia; it's about gratitude for His goodness. It's about how far He's brought us and what we've been through on the way.

As with every transition in life, we each have our own unique experience of coming to know Christ. Some are more dramatic, filled with a lot of "before and after" stories that vividly illustrate a passage from darkness to light. Some are more about a gradual awakening to His love, having always had a sense of His presence, and finally offering themselves fully to Him. Others are somewhere in between. The important part is that, today, we belong to the One who made us, whose grace covers us, and who will never, ever let us go. When we remember this truth, let it be not only for ourselves but for those around us too. Everyone we see—in our families, at work, in our circle of friends, on the street—they're all somewhere on the journey. And they need lots of what we all need: *Grace*. Grace for mistakes. Grace for making selfish decisions. Grace for not knowing better. Grace for knowing better but doing things anyway. One powerful way to share Christ with someone is *grace*. When others would criticize or retaliate, using harsh words or making judgments, we can offer something radically different. Remember: Shame closes hearts. Grace opens them. And if we ever forget that, we need only remember what happened for us when we truly understood that "Amazing Grace" for the first time:

I once was lost
But now am found
Was blind, but now I see.

No matter how long we've been on the journey, may we never forget those first steps and all the things that have transformed along the way—our mindset, our choices, our relationships, our priorities. We haven't always been where we are today and, hopefully, if we continue to walk closely with Him, we will grow even more into tomorrow. There's no finish line in this life, and no competition. We're all holding on to the promise of heaven, doing what we can to bring the kingdom to earth today. So when we look around, let's try to remember that. Who do we know that needs grace the most right now? And how can we offer that priceless gift?

Lord Jesus, I praise You for
the life-changing gift of grace You offer every day.
You accept me as I am and I want to do the same for others.
As I reflect on my own journey,
I am so grateful for all the ways You've been present with me,
guiding and loving me unconditionally.
May my life always reflect that love
in the world around me.

AMEN.

DWELL IN ME,
O BLESSED SPIRIT

ALL OF YOU ARE PART OF THE SAME BODY.
THERE IS ONLY ONE SPIRIT OF GOD,
JUST AS YOU WERE GIVEN ONE HOPE
WHEN YOU WERE CHOSEN TO BE GOD'S PEOPLE.
EPHESIANS 4:4 CEV

Are you ready for a tough (but super helpful!) reminder about relationships? Here goes . . . *Not everyone in your life will understand you 100 percent of the time.* Yes, we all know this deep down. But, no, we don't always remember it (or want to believe it!). *We* are the ones living in these bodies of ours. We are the ones with ourselves 24/7—the only ones who hear our thoughts, feel our feelings, and connect with our Maker in that special way we do. We're so used to being in our own skin that we forget that other people aren't. But it's super important to remember all this when we are walking through something new in our lives. Why? Well, we are each in a unique relationship with our heavenly Father, and that means we each have our own calling, our own understanding of it, and our own way of following through with it. It also means that throughout our lives there will be times when we are called to step out, try something new, or make a change that won't always be understood by everyone around us. Of *course* it's important to reach out to others for wisdom and support along the journey. Of *course* it's wise to prayerfully consider any concerns our loved ones have about the paths we set out on. But, ultimately, we are the ones who will make the decisions and experience whatever unfolds before us as a result. And no matter what that looks like, we can count on a faithful God who will never leave our side. His Spirit is the only One who truly understands us in every way—even when we don't quite understand ourselves! The hymn "Dwell in Me, O Blessed Spirit" is a sweet reminder of His presence within us, loving, teaching, comforting, and guiding:

Dwell in me, O blessed Spirit!
How I need Your help divine!
In the way of life eternal,
Keep, O keep this heart of mine.

This relationship, this eternal connection with Him, will always be the one that matters most in our lives. But none of us is an island; we were made to live in community . . . and the more we surround ourselves with others who know His voice, the more support and assurance we'll enjoy on the journey. Others may not be in our shoes, but they have walked their own paths with the same Guide. They may not understand us perfectly, but they know the One who does. So no matter what we may be called into, let's carefully consider who to call on for support. First, God. Second, those who love and follow Him. We need a balance of good listeners who offer their presence, encouragers who lift us up, and truth-tellers who keep us grounded and nudge us to be honest with ourselves. And when the tables are turned, let us be that voice for others. While we'll never understand everything about each other in this life, the One who created us can reveal things for us to share with one another, helping us to illuminate our paths in unique and inspiring ways.

Heavenly Father, You are the One who sees every part of me and understands me through and through. That's such a blessing for me to know, especially when I'm not even sure I understand myself sometimes! Remind me to turn to You first for guidance in all I do, and show me who I can trust in my life to speak Your truth on the journey.

AMEN.

DWELL IN ME,
O BLESSED SPIRIT

Dwell in me, O blessed Spirit!
How I need Your help divine!
In the way of life eternal,
Keep, O keep this heart of mine.

Dwell in me, O blessed Spirit,
Gracious Teacher, Friend divine!
For the kingdom work that calls me,
O prepare this heart of mine.

Grant to me Your sacred presence;
Then my faith will ne'er decline.
Comfort me and help me onward;
Fill with love this heart of mine.

GOD WILL TAKE CARE OF YOU

*CALL TO ME AND I WILL ANSWER YOU,
AND WILL TELL YOU GREAT AND HIDDEN THINGS
THAT YOU HAVE NOT KNOWN.
JEREMIAH 33:3 ESV*

Comfort zones—we all have them, in our own way. They're like that favorite couch in the living room that we gravitate toward. We know exactly how it feels and where we like to sit on it . . . and once we're there, it can be tough to get back up because it's just. so. cozy. Look up "comfort" and you'll find definitions like "contented," "satisfied," and "relieved." What a wonderful state to be in; why would anyone want to leave it? Well, as we know, we weren't meant to remain in one place forever, at least not in this life! Eventually, whether we like it or not, something will creep in to disrupt our sense of relaxation—a child, a phone call, the sudden realization that we're supposed to be somewhere else doing something else right this minute. Having to leave that comfy place isn't all bad, as most of us have heard that age-old bit of wisdom about having "too much of a good thing." It's true!

And just like what happens when our outer selves lie on couches too long, our inner selves can become comatose too. We have what we need in life, enjoy our circle of influence, get in a daily groove, and do just enough to feel like we're contributing in our little corner of the world. Then we do it all over tomorrow. Life feels pretty okay. But as we've probably observed in life, comfort zones aren't known for producing a lot of growth and change. Unless we step out of our ordinary once in a while, we won't have the opportunity to discover what new things God is up to around (and within!) us. And what happens when we allow some disruption? Lots of unexpected things!

We might feel a nudge to reach out to someone new who is very different from us or to join a group doing something we're passionate about but intimidated by. It could be trying some quiet meditation, when we know how hard it is to sit still and listen. Perhaps it's serving others in an environment that requires us to be vulnerable. We know the nudge when we feel it—He prompts us to step out and try something new as we simultaneously feel the urge to cling to what is safe and familiar. It's okay. There's no judgment. But there *is* our Lord's desire to live and love through us in wonderfully new ways. Daring to trust Him can free us from our predictable agendas and make us available to be used for His greater purposes. The message of the beloved hymn "God Will Take Care of You" gives us the simple reassurance of holding on to a Divine hand regardless of what new steps we may be taking:

All you may need He will provide,
God will take care of you!
Trust Him, and you will be satisfied,
God will take care of you!

It doesn't take monumental courage or some kind of supernatural motivation to try those things that test our limits. All it takes is listening to God. If He calls us to it, He'll give us what we need to try it. Of course, He doesn't condemn us for dragging our feet, but like any loving father, He delights in seeing us grow and experience all He offers us in life. We can do that more and more as we make ourselves available to Him.

Lord, make me uncomfortable in a good way!
I want to experience all You have for me in this life,
and I know that in Christ, I have all the strength, courage,
and motivation I need. Make me sensitive to the voice
of Your Spirit and always willing to answer the call!

AMEN.

WHAT A FRIEND WE HAVE IN JESUS

AND MY GOD WILL SUPPLY
EVERY NEED OF YOURS ACCORDING TO HIS RICHES
IN GLORY IN CHRIST JESUS.
PHILIPPIANS 4:19 ESV

Money is one of those topics that can be tough to talk about, because we all handle it differently. We have different backgrounds and opportunities, priorities about spending it, and beliefs about how it's being handled in the world. There's a reason the Bible has a lot to say about money—we can't get away from it! And it represents a lot more than we often realize. We see this most clearly when there seems to be a money shortage. Whether it's on a national level or something we're dealing with personally, there can be a sense of panic that arises when finances are tight. It can be scary for people who suddenly don't have enough, especially those who don't know where their next meal will come from or how they will be able to provide for their family. Even if we aren't in a desperate situation, we can still feel the stress of having to let go of the comforts and conveniences we've come to depend on or pare down to necessities and adjust our lives in new, disheartening ways. And whether we want to admit it or not, we just can't know what will happen tomorrow even if we're financially comfortable today. Like everything else in life, it's ultimately not in our hands.

It's impossible for us to live in a money bubble. We are connected with the rest of the planet in ways we don't fully realize, and what happens out there affects what happens here—in our homes, our wallets, and every other part of our lives. That's not something for us to fear, though. It's an opportunity for us to draw even closer to our Maker and Provider, especially during those times that feel uncertain. God's Word reminds us that "no one can serve two masters" (Matthew 6:24), and one way we can protect ourselves from losing our peace in times of financial challenge is to remember which Master we serve. The hymn "What a Friend We Have in Jesus" is filled with reminders to trust in God's provision during the changing, challenging times. The first and greatest step we can take when we feel the ground shifting beneath us is to call on Him:

What a friend we have in Jesus,
All our sins and griefs to bear!
What a privilege to carry
Everything to God in prayer.

One message we discover in many old hymns is this reminder: *who God has been in the past is who He will always be*. Those who have gone before us knew what it was to live with a lot or with a little. They've felt exactly what we feel during times of uncertainty, and they knew the comfort that comes from turning toward our Friend and Savior to carry us through. When we face financial insecurity—or anything that causes us to fear tomorrow—we can draw close to the One who holds it all. We can confess our fear, rest in His assurance, listen for His guidance, and watch for ways He provides, just as He has promised.

Lord God, all that I have belongs to You.
I am trusting You as my Provider for everything,
and my finances are in Your hands. Help me to be generous,
to make wise decisions, and to be grateful for all I have.
Help me to loosen my grip on those things I depend upon
for my security. I want to hold tightly to You,
trusting that You see the bigger picture
and know exactly what I need and when.

AMEN.

ABIDE WITH ME

AND SURELY I AM WITH YOU ALWAYS,
TO THE VERY END OF THE AGE.
MATTHEW 28:20 NIV

There are some truly inspiring stories in the world about people who've been faced with limitations and figured out how to thrive in spite of them—maybe someone who was born in a developing country with just enough to survive but who lives with more joy than some of the wealthiest people on the planet. Or perhaps you've heard of someone who sustained a physical injury or even a birth that left them partially disabled—but regardless of their daily challenges, they have a contagious positive spirit. There are people who've been denied a particular opportunity because of their age, gender, or ethnicity, and they've decided to blaze their own trail in another direction. There's a kind of muscle we human beings develop during adversity that can happen in no other way. When we look back, we can often see the ways God has allowed those tough times to shape and strengthen us. We need to be reminded of this often . . . not only when we face life's challenges, but especially when we face new limits. It can be hard to admit that there are things we're no longer able to do for a season—or even longer. We could be facing big financial changes, a health diagnosis, a move to an area that doesn't offer some of our necessities, or even a new way of restrictive eating. Our struggle could be a dream we've held on to for so long, and we finally realize it's just not going to happen like we thought. Watching a proverbial door close can bring up all kinds of feelings—anger, frustration, confusion, and even grieving for something we may never get to experience. If we want to be thrivers rather than mere survivors, we need to be intentional in these times of adversity. We need to tell ourselves the truth about our situation, allowing all those feelings to flow, and then bring everything to Jesus. He understands us more deeply than we do, and He knows exactly what we need to see us through. Most of those people we admire who seem to have found a new kind of joy within their limitations would tell us that there were (and sometimes still are!) moments when they just wanted to give up. Those are the moments when we most need the strength of our Savior. "Abide with Me" has comforted people throughout generations with its reminder of His constant presence, especially in the toughest times:

Abide with me: fast falls the eventide;
The darkness deepens: Lord, with me abide!
When other helpers fail and comforts flee,
Help of the helpless, O, abide with me!

This is a message not only for our own heart, but also for those around us. We all need reminders that our Maker doesn't sit far away, watching things unfold. He abides *with* us. His love for us is active and present through our brightest days and our darkest nights. That's a vital part of the gospel we share. Emmanuel, "God with us," is here to see us through.

Jesus, it's hard when things in life don't happen
the way I'm hoping or feel they should.
I know I can't see the big picture like You can,
and I get discouraged sometimes.
I need Your greater vision in those moments,
to remind me that another door will always open . . .
maybe even where I least expect it.
I lift up everyone who's feeling limited in their own way today.
May we all remember that our ultimate happiness is
found not in our circumstances but in You.

AMEN.

THERE SHALL BE SHOWERS OF BLESSING

FINALLY, BROTHERS, WHATEVER IS TRUE, WHATEVER IS HONORABLE, WHATEVER IS JUST, WHATEVER IS PURE, WHATEVER IS LOVELY, WHATEVER IS COMMENDABLE, IF THERE IS ANY EXCELLENCE, IF THERE IS ANYTHING WORTHY OF PRAISE, THINK ABOUT THESE THINGS. PHILIPPIANS 4:8 ESV

We all have our own favorite seasons of the year, for our own reasons. The "spring" people often name that feeling of hope they get as the world comes to life: nature's bright colors returning and new beginnings happening after months of cold and dark. Summer fans love the warmth and the sunshine; long, lazy days; water fun; and slower schedules. Fall folks welcome the cooler air; the vibrant, changing leaves; Crock-Pot recipes; and the return of favorite sports. And among the many "winter" joys are snowy days, cozy nights, blazing fires, cocoa, and comfort food in the kitchen. It's funny that the same season can appear at the top of one person's list and sit at the bottom of another's. We all have our preferences—that's just part of our uniqueness as God's creation. But there's an interesting thing that happens once we decide that something is our favorite. We start to focus on all the wonderful details about it, and those less-than-desirable aspects kind of fade into the background. Sure, those summer people love their sunshine, but they quickly forget that, some days, the heat can be sweltering. As the winter folks think of building snowmen, they somehow dismiss the time spent clearing ice from windshields and mounds of snow from the driveway. In other words, the more we focus on the good stuff, the less we see of anything else. This can be true about our seasons of life too.

As the years pass, we go from living at home to making it in the "real world," raising babies to reining in high schoolers, or juggling a busy career to enjoying (a sometimes-even-busier!) retirement, and everything in between. When we reflect on the times we've lived through, what do we remember most? Our snapshots of memories are created by what we choose to focus on. What we're most mindful of in each season of life will always stand out on the pages of our history. God's Word reminds us that the way we experience life is always within our power. We're invited to give thanks in all circumstances and to set our minds on things above. Why? Because our Maker knows that's where our true joy lies. The hymn "There Shall Be Showers of Blessing" celebrates the promises God has given to bless us, in every season:

> *There shall be showers of blessing:*
> *This is the promise of love;*
> *There shall be seasons refreshing,*
> *Sent from the Savior above.*

Just as we like to do with our favorite time of the year, we can choose to focus on the good during any season of life. This is how we become more and more aware of God's blessings. They're never scarce; we just miss them sometimes. One of the secrets to a rich and satisfying life is to love what *is*, not to wait for what *will be*. We've heard it said that happiness doesn't happen tomorrow; it can only be found in today. Whatever age or stage of life you're experiencing now is sure to bring its own unique challenges and blessings. Whichever you choose to focus on is what you'll remember most when you look back at these years.

Father, thank You for being present with me in every season of life and inviting me to see those blessings You're constantly giving. Open my eyes and heart to all the goodness I'm not yet aware of. Help me live with joy and gratitude so that when I look back on this time, I'll find countless reasons to smile.

AMEN.

HAVE THINE OWN WAY, LORD

IMITATE GOD, THEREFORE, IN EVERYTHING YOU DO,
BECAUSE YOU ARE HIS DEAR CHILDREN.
LIVE A LIFE FILLED WITH LOVE,
FOLLOWING THE EXAMPLE OF CHRIST.
HE LOVED US AND OFFERED HIMSELF
AS A SACRIFICE FOR US, A PLEASING AROMA TO GOD.
EPHESIANS 5:1-2 NLT

At some point in life, you've probably heard the phrase "my biggest fan." Maybe someone has introduced you to their mother, who has always shown up to support them in everything they do. Or they tell you about a teacher or a coach who believed in them wholeheartedly and always encouraged them to "go for it." Maybe *you've* been someone's biggest fan—a younger relative or any loved one who has needed some cheering on. There's nothing like knowing that someone in our lives is truly in our corner for the long haul—no matter what we try, no matter who else believes in us, and no matter what the outcome may be. Showing up with support, even when it's inconvenient and *especially* when the odds seem to be stacked against—that's love in action.

When we think about how we can serve each other, being an encourager is one role any of us can play. Maybe we know someone right now who is trying something new or finally following a lifelong dream or taking steps toward a goal that seems impossible to the world (yet they refuse to give up). We may admire others' efforts from afar, but it's easy to forget how hard it is to be in their shoes. Sometimes it takes every ounce of courage a person has to make that leap. We serve a God whose heart is so tender toward those in a vulnerable place—the underdogs, the hope-filled souls giving it all they have, the ones who keep trying despite what the world believes about their chances. A powerful way we can share His love is by reaching out to those who need that voice of encouragement. Regardless of the outcome, those precious people need to know that they are not forgotten; they are treasured merely for who they are, no matter what they accomplish. If we want people to see Jesus when they look at us, we have to ask Him how He wants to show up for them and then be willing to show up for them in His Name. As the hymn "Have Thine Own Way, Lord" reminds us, the more we surrender our lives to Him, the more we will reflect His love:

Have Thine own way, Lord! Have Thine own way!
Hold o'er my being absolute sway.
Fill with Thy Spirit till all shall see
Christ only, always, living in me!

Our loving Father knows just who needs to see Christ in us today. He knows who's trying to find the courage to step into something new. He knows who feels secretly defeated, who needs someone to cheer them on, and who could use a word of encouragement at just the right time. So let's sit in His presence as often as we can and open our heart to volunteer to be ambassadors of His love in a world that needs it desperately. It's one of the greatest earthly joys we'll ever know.

Jesus, when I pray for others, I need to remember that
sometimes You call me to help answer those prayers!
I know there are people in my life right now who need
to be encouraged or hear they're not alone.
Draw me toward them, Lord. I want my life
to reflect Your love in whatever way You lead me.

AMEN.

SING PRAISE TO GOD WHO REIGNS ABOVE

AND I AM CERTAIN THAT GOD,
WHO BEGAN THE GOOD WORK WITHIN YOU,
WILL CONTINUE HIS WORK UNTIL IT IS FINALLY FINISHED
ON THE DAY WHEN CHRIST JESUS RETURNS.
PHILIPPIANS 1:6 NLT

Milestone birthdays—they bring mixed feelings as we celebrate lives, ponder our purposes, reflect on days gone by, and anticipate what is to come. Depending on where and when we grew up, different years are marked as ones most significant. Often thirteen is a big milestone, nudging us out of childhood and into those full-blown teen years. "Sweet sixteen" marks our gradual transition into adulthood, and eighteen or twenty-one seals the deal. By the time we hit thirty, we may be starting to look behind us and marveling at how quickly the years have flown. Forty arrives with family and friends teasing us about growing older (even if we feel ageless inside!). And on it goes. Of course, the origin of the word *milestones* is just what we'd expect—a series of markers placed along a road to indicate how far a person has traveled. When we see our lives like that—as a road with a beginning and an end—it makes sense to anticipate those milestone years ahead in the distance. Of course, the world tells us what to expect and strongly suggests how we behave at any given age. We *should* feel this way at twenty, have *this* accomplished by thirty, not wear *that* after forty . . . you get the idea. But if you think about it on a spiritual level, the life Jesus calls us into really isn't linear at all. The world's markers no longer apply and we don't have to worry about what's over the next hill (even though we sometimes do!). We don't even have to consider what the person beside us is doing at that age. The progression of our life in Christ is about depth much more than distance. It's about diving into His purpose for us today, not running to keep ahead of the herd tomorrow. It's about leaning into His love for us right here and now, not looking for validation in the next relationship or accomplishment down the road.

The hymn "Sing Praise to God Who Reigns Above" has been played and sung on countless occasions throughout the years. It reminds us of this truth: no matter where we are in life, He is the only marker we will ever need, the one we will never move beyond. Years pass and birthdays come and go, but our true life will always be found in Him:

> Sing praise to God who reigns above,
> The God of all creation,
> The God of power, the God of love,
> The God of our salvation.

Maybe you have a milestone coming up or know someone who does. Or maybe you've just noticed how often we can feel the burden of the world's standards and expectations as we age. Always remember that the most significant point is the current moment, right where you are, because that's where He will always be. As the days turn to weeks to months to years, life will bring what it will bring for us. And the more we rest in Him, the more we will be ready to embrace each day with courage and grace at any age.

Lord Jesus, You are all I will ever need.
Forgive me for those times I find myself looking elsewhere
for what can only be found in You.
Nothing that I celebrate in this life will ever come close
to the marvelous reality of knowing You each day.
When I become fearful about the future, bring me back to now,
where You are and will always be.

AMEN.

I HEARD THE VOICE OF JESUS SAY

BUT THANKS BE TO GOD!
HE GIVES US THE VICTORY
THROUGH OUR LORD JESUS CHRIST.
I CORINTHIANS 15:57 NIV

It's easy to take our bodies for granted when things are running smoothly. If we're blessed with sight, we have the gift of opening our eyes to the world's beauty each morning. If we're able to walk, our legs carry us out into the kitchen for that first sip of something wonderful (which we've been given the taste buds to enjoy!). Most parts of us just do their thing, and we get to be along for the ride. So when something breaks down, it may surprise us and will likely annoy us, and if it's a big-enough deal, it might even make us a little fearful. Our health matters more than we often realize, and when it becomes a struggle, we're awakened again to the blessing that it is. We're reminded that God has given us one body to spend this life in, and we can choose to be grateful for it every day. Moreover, He didn't just *create* these bodies; He chose to inhabit one. Jesus knows how the earth feels beneath our feet and how the heart feels beating in the chest. He knows what it's like to be hungry and thirsty, exhausted and hurt, broken in ways most of us will never have to know. And the healing He offers is for all of it—not just our physical selves, but our spirits too. That's the message of the hymn "I Heard the Voice of Jesus Say":

> *I heard the voice of Jesus say,*
> *"Behold, I freely give*
> *The living water, thirsty one;*
> *Stoop down and drink and live."*

We've all been touched by brokenness in some way. Whether it be our own or that of someone we love, we just want all of it to be okay again. We pray for healing, and maybe it comes quickly. Or it might take much longer than we hoped. Maybe we're still hoping, asking the Lord to get us through one more day. It can be hard, wondering why things aren't changing, and it can be easy to become frustrated and discouraged as we focus on that one thing we need and forget about all we still have in the moment.

Something powerful that we can do for ourselves in those times is to stop and look at what *is* working—what *is* good in our lives right now. That doesn't mean we have to deny the pain we're feeling, but finding something to be grateful for in the midst of it all can make a big difference. And there's one thing we can always focus on to bring us joy . . . the gift we've been given in Christ. The victory we sing of may not be manifested in the way we want right then, but it is there regardless because of who He has been and will always be for us, as He sustains us even now in ways we don't realize. When we have one of those I-just-can't-do-it-anymore days, let's ask Him to remind us of all He's already done. "It is finished," as He promised (see John 19:30). All we will ever need is found in Him. And whether it be in this life or the next, we will experience that victory in every ounce of our being. Today, let's find it in all the places we can and continue to trust Him for the healing we need.

Jesus, thank You for being my Healer in every way.
Thank You for walking this earth so that You could
intimately know what it feels like to be human.
Help me appreciate all those blessings that I take for granted
most days. Just to be alive is an indescribable gift!

AMEN.

BEFORE THE THRONE
OF GOD ABOVE

GOD DECIDED IN ADVANCE TO ADOPT US
INTO HIS OWN FAMILY BY BRINGING US
TO HIMSELF THROUGH JESUS CHRIST.
EPHESIANS 1:5 NLT

God's heart for those in need is evident throughout His Word. He calls us in many ways to be His hands and feet in the world for those who can't care for themselves. And while that looks different for each of us, for some it will include adoption. What a wonderful and life-changing decision, to give a child the gift of a forever family. Even if we aren't the ones who've made that choice, we probably know someone who has. And while we may not be in their so-called shoes, we can always offer our support and encouragement as they answer the call to adopt. When someone takes a child into their home and heart, they're choosing to provide something that was never required of them. Their actions are showing that child, "You weren't born to me, but now I choose to call you mine, forever." It's one of the most beautiful examples of sacrificial love that we can witness.

Of course, the bonds we share with birth children are infinitely precious, but an adopted child represents something *uniquely* precious. It is an illustration of our infinite worth as human beings, regardless of who we are or how we began. It's about recognizing that we belong to each other as God's creations, and it's about deciding to embody the truth of it in a real and lasting way. Adoption is one of the most touching displays of His tender love for us because He chose us, just as adoptive parents choose children who need them. Ephesians 1:5 reminds us, "God decided in advance to adopt us into his own family by bringing us to Himself through Jesus Christ. This is what He wanted to do, and it gave Him great pleasure" (NLT).

Just like many of the steps the Spirit nudges us to take in life, adoption is not easy. Each family has its unique story, but most of them involve some significant financial and emotional adjustment. There are stories of waiting, hoping, heartbreaking disappointment, and indescribable joy, such as when that last legal step is taken and the first real cuddle or hug is given. There can be rough beginnings, unexpected delights, times of doubt and frustration, and moments when it's so clear that God's plan for a specific child was to be with one certain family all along. What that family becomes for that child is a reflection of who God is for us. The One to whom we belong, the home we can always return to, the Father who says to us, in essence, "I choose you, just as you are, forever." This truth is captured in the hymn "Before the Throne of God Above":

My name is graven on His hands;
My name is written on His heart.
I know that while in heav'n He stands;
No tongue can bid me thence depart.

Let's remember this wonderful truth when we encounter adoptive families in our schools, churches, and communities. (And maybe we, ourselves, are living that life!) We are looking at a reflection of God's generous love for us—offered freely, never earned, and always there to remind us that we are part of a forever family.

Father God, being adopted into Your family is the greatest gift
of my life. When someone chooses to open their home
and heart to a child in need, may I always remember
that it's a reflection of what You've done for me.
And whenever You call me to support someone in need,
I want to offer all I have.

AMEN.

ALL THINGS BRIGHT AND BEAUTIFUL

FOR BY HIM ALL THINGS WERE CREATED,
BOTH IN THE HEAVENS AND ON EARTH,
VISIBLE AND INVISIBLE, WHETHER THRONES,
OR DOMINIONS, OR RULERS, OR AUTHORITIES—
ALL THINGS HAVE BEEN CREATED
THROUGH HIM AND FOR HIM.
COLOSSIANS 1:16 NASB

Way back in that nostalgic decade we call "the '80s," a unique event took place that connected over five million people across the United States. Before smart phones, before social media, before virtual meetings, we had . . . *Hands Across America*. It was a human chain that stretched throughout parts of the country from New York to California, simply by holding hands. It was also a remarkable illustration of how we are all connected . . . coast to coast, country to country, even one side of this great big earth to the other, theoretically. What we do affects people we can't see—and may *never* see in this life. Not only that, but what we do affects this place where we live, this beautiful globe God created for us to inhabit and enjoy.

Some of us are more aware of that truth and often think about the ripple effect of the choices we make, whether it be what businesses we frequent, what organizations we contribute to, what we do to care for our little corner of the earth, or how we treat both our loved ones and strangers alike. That smile we share can make its way many miles, passed from one person to another. In the same way, that careless thing said in anger can cast a shadow that reaches much further than we might imagine. And when we do even the smallest thing to care for God's creation, it can make a bigger difference than we know. It's easy to forget sometimes that we're part of this great big world in ways we don't think about. But when the weight of that truth does impact us, we can always take a step or make a change. It doesn't have to be a big thing. We can ask the Lord where we might do one small thing to start a ripple of goodness. We can take some quiet time to consider our daily lives and how we interact with creation (whether that be people, plants, or animals). What God made in the beginning He called "good," and we honor Him when we care for it—all of it.

The words to the hymn "All Things Bright and Beautiful" have been cherished through generations by adults and children alike. They offer us a simple but powerful reminder that we are connected with, and surrounded by, His wonderful work:

All things bright and beautiful,
All creatures great and small,
All things wise and wonderful,
The Lord God made them all.

Whether it's a simple change in our daily routine or a bigger shift to how we impact the world around us, every little step we take matters to our Maker. And though we will never really know the end result of our actions in this life (because they will likely reach much further than we could ever see!), we can still find joy in it all, knowing that we do it out of love and gratitude for Him.

Lord, what a wondrous world You've created for us to inhabit
and enjoy! I want to remember every day how interconnected
we are with each other and with all You have made.
I want to honor You by finding ways to share Your love and
care for Your creation however I'm able. I know that even the
smallest step I take for the good of all matters infinitely to You.

AMEN.

ALL THINGS BRIGHT
AND BEAUTIFUL

All things bright and beautiful,
All creatures great and small,
All things wise and wonderful,
The Lord God made them all.

Each little flow'r that opens,
Each little bird that sings,
God made their glowing colors,
God made their tiny wings.

The purple-headed mountain,
The river running by,
The sunset, and the morning
That brightens up the sky;

The cold wind in the winter,
The pleasant summer sun,
The ripe fruits in the garden,
God made them, ev'ry one.

God gave us eyes to see them,
And lips that we might tell
How great is God Almighty,
Who has made all things well.

SOFTLY AND TENDERLY, JESUS IS CALLING

AND HE SAID, "MY PRESENCE SHALL GO WITH YOU,
AND I WILL GIVE YOU REST."
EXODUS 33:14 NASB

The hymn "Softly and Tenderly, Jesus Is Calling" has been cherished by many through the years as they've walked through tough times, seeking the peace and assurance that only God can give. We've all had our own difficult seasons—facing doubt or uncertainty, exhaustion, confusion, fear, and maybe even the grief of saying goodbye to a loved one as they left this world and entered their heavenly home. The hymn comforts us with Jesus's wonderful, open invitation to all of us:

> Come home, come home;
> You who are weary, come home;
> Earnestly, tenderly, Jesus is calling,
> Calling, O sinner, come home!

When we enter our later years of life, this message can bring special comfort as we're reminded that this world is not our final destination—but the loving embrace of our Savior is. It's not just a message about the "sweet by and by," though. This hymn's words are relevant to any of us on the journey with Jesus at any time. He's calling us home to Himself right now, every day, in *this* life. And where is that home? A church building, a temple, or some other holy place set aside for worship and prayer? We know the answer. That dwelling is within us, where He now lives by His Spirit. This means that as lost as we feel sometimes, as discouraged with what's happening in the world around us, as fearful as we can be about the changes life may bring . . . we have a quiet place to return to, a shelter from the storm, a sense of peace that is just a breath away. We have a loving, caring Presence that resides within us, and all we have to do is become aware of Him again.

Have you noticed how many forces are out there working hard to pull us out of that peace and away from our heart? Temptations, distractions, media commentators telling us what we *should* be doing or thinking about. There's a lot out there vying for our attention, and much of it leaves us feeling separated from our true God-created selves. But we know exactly who we are and whose we are; we just forget sometimes. We belong to Christ, and that is the beginning and the end of everything for us. "In Him we live and move and have our being" (Acts 17:28 NIV). There is no other. No matter what else changes in our lives, no matter what choices or mistakes we make, how off course we find ourselves or how far away we wander, *who He is for us will never change*. Are you tired? Frustrated? Lonely? Fearful about what is ahead? "Come home," He says. We are perfectly welcome just as we are, and we are only one moment away from that awareness of His presence. Sit in a quiet place when you can. Allow your mind to be still and your thoughts to rest on Him. Come back to yourself. In doing so, you will come home to the One who calls you from within even now.

Lord Jesus, I want to say yes to Your invitation every day.
Thank You for being with me in every way—
and for the peace that fills my heart
when I remember that You'll never leave me.
May I become increasingly more conscious of Your presence
and less fearful about whatever I face in life.
Wherever I go, I know that I will always find
my true home in You.

AMEN.

THIS IS MY FATHER'S WORLD

BUT THE LORD OUR GOD IS
MERCIFUL AND FORGIVING....
DANIEL 9:9 NLT

Do you ever stop and think about all the voices in the world that are shouting for your attention at any moment? All the marketing messages trying to pull you this way or that, the friends who feel strongly about something, the trends that grow so quickly that herds of people start to wear the same color or use the same expression seemingly overnight. There's a lot of what we call *influence* out there. In fact, these days, a person can make a lot of money as an "influencer." (If you're not a big social-media fan, an influencer is someone with considerable power to affect the decisions of their online audience.) It's easy to find ourselves wondering, *Who's really running the show these days?* or *Whose world is this, anyway?* But we know whose it is. No matter how loud the crowd becomes, no matter what spiritual forces attempt to take over and derail the whole thing, our Maker holds it all in His hands. He's never surprised, disappointed, or concerned with what's happening; He knows exactly where it's all going and how. The hymn "This Is My Father's World" inspires us to remember that:

> *This is my Father's world:*
> *Why should my heart be sad?*
> *The Lord is King: let the heavens ring!*
> *God reigns; let earth be glad!*

But here's the thing: We humans can be easily influenced. We're part of this world, even if we sometimes wish we weren't. We are swimming in this river called "life," and the current can be strong. It's likely there will be moments when we look up and wonder how we drifted so far or how we got so tangled up in something we never saw coming. These are the times we wish we had been more aware, sooner, of how something might affect us downstream. They say hindsight is 20/20, but foresight . . . not so much.

Just remember this: We are imperfect people doing our best to navigate an imperfect world. Sometimes we just lose our way. We miss the Spirit's nudge to pay attention, or we hear that still, small voice and forge ahead anyway. We may spend our time beating ourselves up about getting off course and making "that" choice, wondering how we could let the circumstance or relationship affect our heart and mind so negatively. But every moment we lose to guilt and shame is a moment that could have held peace and joy for us. And our heavenly Father doesn't ask us to sit and resent ourselves for a while before we come to Him again. He doesn't dole out grace every so often, like only when we *really* deserve it. Remember the words of Jesus in Matthew 11:28, "Come to Me . . ." That's a forever-open invitation. When the world feels overwhelming . . . when we realize that we need to change course . . . when we would condemn ourselves—let us remember that "God did not send His Son into the world to condemn the world, but to save the world through Him" (John 3:17 NIV). That's about you and me and all of us who would come to Him today. In our Father's world, grace will always abound.

Jesus, I just lose my way sometimes. I get swept up in that rushing river of life and end up regretting it. I don't want to waste the precious time You've given me by living under a cloud of guilt and shame. When I've drifted, I need to hear that tender voice of Your Spirit calling me home to Yourself, again and again. Thank You for loving me no matter what.

AMEN.

JESUS PAID IT ALL

TURN TO ME AND BE GRACIOUS TO ME,
FOR I AM LONELY AND AFFLICTED.
PSALM 25:16 NIV

Most of us at some point in our lives have felt something we'd describe as loneliness. It may have had to do with where we live or how our daily life was structured. It may have been from struggles in our relationships or even our choice to tuck ourselves away from the world for whatever reason. Sometimes we're aware of our loneliness, and other times it just shows up as a gnawing sense of sadness that we can't identify the source of. As Christ followers, we know that human beings were made for connection—and not just the physical kind, but the spiritual kind that can't be seen or measured from the outside. Even the most introverted among us can feel deeply connected all by herself, and even the most extroverted can feel lonely in a crowd. That's because loneliness isn't about whether people are around us. It's something that happens within us . . . a kind of emptiness we carry that longs to be filled. We may try all sorts of ways to ease the ache. But from the beginning, long before we ever arrived on the scene, our God was planning for the fulfillment of all humankind. He knew that in this broken world, something deep within us would miss Him. And whether we realized what was making us feel so empty, nothing would satisfy that longing but Christ Himself. The hymn "Jesus Paid It All" celebrates all He is for us. As we sing those words, we can be reminded that there is nothing more we need but to be found in Him:

> *I hear the Savior say,*
> *"Thy strength indeed is small,*
> *Child of weakness, watch and pray,*
> *Find in Me thine all in all."*

We know that this world is not our true home. And as wonderful as our life in Christ can be, we will all go through periods of feeling needier and less connected, more insecure and less fulfilled. During those times, it's important to remind ourselves that He always provides ways to help us sense His love and nearness, and those ways are unique to each of us. So when we encounter a time or a season of loneliness, we can remember to turn to Him first. While it may be our natural inclination to reach for a relationship or that thing that might help us feel "full" again, let's ask Him where we can experience His presence more deeply. It could be spending more time in His Word, reflecting on His promises. Maybe there's someone in our lives He's nudging us to draw closer to, knowing how our connection will help us both to know Him in new ways. Perhaps there's something in nature that helps us feel His heart through creation. As we've all learned, there will be ups and downs—but let us never forget that through His death and resurrection, we are complete and forever found in Him. Even on the days when we forget it, and even when we find ourselves feeling forgotten, we are never more than a thought, a breath, or a prayer away from the One who *is* all and is *in* all.

Heavenly Father, sometimes I feel a sense of loneliness
or emptiness and I don't even know why.
But I do know that You are always willing
to comfort my heart when I come to You.
Help me to see more clearly what's happening within me.
Instead of reaching for a "fix,"
help me turn to You during those times.
I want to feel the warmth and tenderness
of Your constant presence.

AMEN.

ROCK OF AGES

YOU ARE THE GOD WHO SEES ME.
GENESIS 16:13 NIV

Imagine watching a child you love trying really hard to do something—create a piece of art or practice a sport, for example— or a toddler concentrating intently on taking those first wobbly steps across the room. We delight in watching their process. Whether they color outside the lines or stay in them, whether they strike out or get to slide into home, whether they make it one step or ten . . . it doesn't change our love for them one ounce. In fact, as we watch them struggle, sometimes it feels as if our heart grows bigger. We want to see them succeed—not so that they can impress us or earn our affection, but because we know what is happening within them. We want them to truly enjoy their accomplishments, to grow in confidence, and to be open to trying new things in life.

We know that what the world may call "failure" is actually part of something much bigger: a process that teaches them, strengthens them, and inspires them to get up and keep trying. Of course, it always helps to have someone by their side, cheering them on. Even if we can't fix something or finish it for them, we can remind them of their worth and let them know that it doesn't matter how many times they have to try; we believe in them, and we aren't going anywhere. We will be there looking over their shoulder proudly, there in the bleachers, there holding out a hand in case they need to steady themselves. The well-known hymn "Rock of Ages" is a beautiful illustration of Christ's unwavering presence in the lives of His children, regardless of what we bring, how we perform, or whether we feel worthy:

> *Not the labor of my hands*
> *Can fulfill Thy law's demands;*

Could my zeal no respite know,
Could my tears forever flow,
All could not atone,
Thou must save, and Thou alone.

What a relief to understand how completely safe and accepted we are in Him. Does His grace make us want to fail? Does it make us want to take advantage of His infinite love for us? Of course not. When our heart is His, our greatest desire is to respond to His goodness by giving our love right back. And we know that it's not going to be perfect. We're going to color outside the lines sometimes and strike out sometimes and lose our balance sometimes. But the beautiful thing about being a child of God is that we do not live under a condemning gaze. We live beneath the tender gaze of a loving Father. Have you been feeling pressure to perform? To do enough, be enough, or prove yourself in any way? That may be how the world operates, but not the kingdom. Let this be a gentle reminder that in Christ, "it is finished" (John 19:30). There is nothing more to do but love Him back in our own imperfect way. Whether you need to hear this now or in the future: you are complete in Him.

Lord, it's such a relief when I let go of
striving, proving, and performing.
The thought of You as my loving Father,
watching over me tenderly,
fills my heart with warmth and gratitude.
No matter what I attempt to do in this life,
may I rest in the knowledge that I am already loved,
accepted, and complete in Christ.
Every part of me is Yours.

AMEN.

NEW EVERY MORNING
IS THE LOVE

I WILL SING ALOUD
OF YOUR STEADFAST LOVE
IN THE MORNING.
PSALM 59:16 ESV

We all go through seasons in life that feel a little chaotic and a lot unsettled. There may be some uncertain things with our job; a loved one is facing a challenge; financial shifts are happening; we're working through some big family decisions . . . the possibilities are endless. Life, as we all know, is ever changing and often unpredictable, so we learn to "roll with it" as best we can. However, that's not always easy, and whatever we can do to find peace—especially during extra-anxious days—will surely help to see us through. If you think about it, morning is where it all starts. The way we start the morning can set the tone for the whole day. If we wake up refreshed and savor a few moments of peace, there's a good chance we'll have more calm in our day. If we jump out of bed and begin running from thing to thing, it's likely that more chaos will ensue as the hours unfold. As the sun rises, we can visualize the day as an empty canvas. The hymn "New Every Morning is the Love" paints a picture of that wonderful newness we're invited to experience:

> *New every morning is the love*
> *Our wakening and uprising prove;*
> *Through sleep and darkness safely brought,*
> *Restored to life and power and thought.*

We have a choice the moment we open our eyes. We can see the potential in that canvas before us, lift our heart in praise for another day of life, and begin painting with bright colors . . . or we can start to fill it with the darker hues of yesterday's worries and frustrations, leaving little room for the joys God has waiting for us to discover today. Just as anything we do daily, we form habits over time without realizing it. Maybe jumping anxiously out of bed and diving directly into our to-do list has become second nature.

How do *you* begin your mornings? Is there something small you'd like to change; if so, why not try it tomorrow? If this is a season of rougher waters in your life, you'll benefit from a more peaceful beginning to the day. If things aren't currently all that difficult, you'll be creating a new habit for when you need it most. Even a small step taken prayerfully can make a big difference. Try sitting quietly for ten minutes with Jesus and a mug of something warm and wonderful. Or keep a journal by the bed to jot down any worries that come to mind once you open your eyes; you can entrust everything to His care. A little walk outside, a few minutes of prayer over your still-sleeping children, or a candle lit in the kitchen can remind you of God's presence throughout the day. Above all, consider asking the Holy Spirit whether He has something in mind for you as you begin your morning.

Lord, every morning You give me
the marvelous gift of an empty canvas.
I know that I don't always see it that way
when I'm rushing right into the day.
I forget that I have the freedom to choose
how I will experience this day.
I want to take a moment to slow down,
clear my vision, and tune into Your Spirit.
How can that happen for me?
May I always look to You first to set the tone for my days.

AMEN.

STANDING ON THE PROMISES

*AS IRON SHARPENS IRON,
SO ONE PERSON SHARPENS ANOTHER.
PROVERBS 27:17 NIV*

Relationships are among God's greatest blessings on this journey of life. They bring us joy, give us heart-filling experiences of connection, and help us to become more like Jesus. There are ways we grow through our relationships with others that we would never grow on our own. But we all know the unfortunate truth about growth: *it can hurt!* If trees could talk, they'd surely tell us that sprouting from a tiny seed into a mighty oak was not comfortable. And just ask a kid who's been awakened by growing pains in the night—when big change is happening, it can definitely be felt!

Back to relationships: sometimes they hurt because they're growing us. When our heart is out there, when we've shared our lives and allowed ourselves to be vulnerable, and then we hit a rough patch . . . it can leave us feeling frustrated, disappointed, and a little (or a lot!) insecure. When that happens, we're invited to draw close to Jesus and pour out our heart to Him. As we pray for ourselves and for the other person, we should remember that our side of the story is the one we know best and there's always more going on than we can see. Perhaps they were intentionally hurtful, or maybe they made a mistake they deeply regret. Maybe anger took over a conversation and harsh words were said. Or maybe our feelings were hurt and the other person has no idea what they did to cause it. Whatever it is, we can always make room for grace. And grace happens when we allow the Holy Spirit to do His thing—that wonderful healing work in our hearts that we're not able to do on our own.

These are the times when we remember that we're all human, all capable of hurting and disappointing one another. These are also the times when we remember that the only relationship we have in this life that will never fail us is the one we have with our Savior. The promises He gives us will never be revoked; His love will never waver for a moment; and He is our solid place to stand when other connections feel less than dependable. The words to the hymn "Standing on the Promises" remind us of this beautiful truth:

Standing on the promises I cannot fall,
List'ning every moment to the Spirit's call.
Resting in my Savior as my all in all,
Standing on the promises of God.

What are some of those promises concerning our relationships? When we love each other deeply, a multitude of sins will be covered (I Peter 4:8). When we are "quick to listen, slow to speak and slow to become angry" (James 1:19 NIV), we become more like Christ. When we humble ourselves, God has promised to lift us up (James 4:10). The more security we find in our relationship with Jesus, the less insecurity we will feel in our connections with everyone else. And when big conflicts arise, sometimes it's about forgiving and reconciling. Other times it's about forgiving and moving on, acknowledging that this relationship was intended just for a season in our lives. But *every* time, it's about drawing closer to Christ— experiencing His love for us in deeper ways and learning to keep our heart open to Him no matter what happens with those around us.

Father, thank You for giving us the gift of relationship. We need
each other as we journey through this life, but even more than
that, we need You. All my connections are in Your hands,
and I pray that each of them would help me come to know
You more deeply and live like Christ more fully.

AMEN.

I SHALL NOT BE MOVED

BUT BLESSED IS THE ONE WHO TRUSTS IN THE LORD,
WHOSE CONFIDENCE IS IN HIM.
THEY WILL BE LIKE A TREE PLANTED BY THE WATER
THAT SENDS OUT ITS ROOTS BY THE STREAM.
IT DOES NOT FEAR WHEN HEAT COMES;
ITS LEAVES ARE ALWAYS GREEN.
IT HAS NO WORRIES IN A YEAR OF DROUGHT
AND NEVER FAILS TO BEAR FRUIT.
JEREMIAH 17:7-8 NIV

"I Shall Not Be Moved" is an old gospel hymn that celebrates the strength and security we find in Christ regardless of what we face in life. It describes believers as trees planted by the water, which, as we read in Psalm 1:3, will bear "luscious fruit each season without fail. Their leaves shall never wither, and all they do shall prosper" (TLB). We can imagine our spiritual brothers and sisters down through the years, singing these words as they endured even the most challenging times:

> In His love abiding, I shall not be moved
> And in Him confiding, I shall not be moved
> Just like a tree that's planted by the waters,
> I shall not be moved.

Many of us have felt the truth of this message in our own lives. We look back and see all the ways our loving Father has provided for us, and it gives us hope and assurance for the journey ahead. When times of doubt, fear, or uncertainty come, we know that we don't have to panic the way the world around us often does. We only need to remember whose we are and what that means. In Christ, we are children of God (John 1:12) and a temple of the Holy Spirit

(I Corinthians 6:19). Our every need is supplied (Philippians 4:19), and we are free from the law of sin and death (Romans 8:2). If these things are true, then what have we to fear?

Have you ever watched someone of admirable faith walk through a really tough time—and you marveled at the peace she seemed to carry within despite her circumstances? What others witnessed in those moments was a reflection of that tree rooted firmly in a place where it had all the nourishment it needed. That person knew that whatever she needed to see her through would be provided by her Maker. She stood firm in the truth that His supply is unlimited and that she belongs to Him eternally. Most likely, she learned to lean on Him through experience. That's how we learn it too. The next time we're faced with something that feels overwhelming and out of our control, we can remember that we, too, are firmly rooted in Him. The more we go experience, the more opportunity we have to draw close and discover how very real His presence is and how deeply He cares for the details of our lives.

Think about what else we see when we look at a tree that's thriving. We see other forms of life finding shelter within and beneath its branches. As we learn to trust Him more and more, others will find strength in that. They will look to us and see an illustration of His provision. It will build their faith too, and when they face their own tough times, they'll be encouraged to do what we did: place their unwavering trust in God, draw all they need from His promises, and stand firm, knowing that their roots are constantly nourished by His love.

Father, thank You for providing, nurturing, supporting,
protecting, and loving me in the ways that only You can.
May the roots of my faith grow ever deeper in You and
the branches of my life stretch further toward those who need
to see Your love in action. When tough times come,
remind me that I am eternally secure in You.

AMEN.

PRECIOUS MEMORIES

BUT MARY KEPT ALL THESE THINGS IN HER HEART
AND THOUGHT ABOUT THEM OFTEN.
LUKE 2:19 NLT

The words of the hymn "Precious Memories" have been deeply felt over the years by so many who have had to say goodbye to someone dear to them. Whether it happened last week, last year, or much further in the past, we may find ourselves surprised when a sudden memory of those loved ones comes to mind. It can warm our heart and bring a sense of sadness all at once—the true definition of "bittersweet":

> As I travel on life's pathway,
> Know not what the years may hold;
> As I ponder, hope grows fonder,
> Precious mem'ries flood my soul.

Think about this: there has never been a time that we have lived without memories. From our very first years of life as our minds began to mature, we were able to recall things that happened in the past (even if the "past" didn't stretch very far back at that point!). Of course, not every part of our stories is pleasant to remember, but for those parts we *do* want to hold on to, we have the blessing of tucking them away to bring them out when we need them the most. What a gift God has given us in memories! It's hard to imagine our lives without them, and it's easy to take them for granted. But when we need them most, we realize the healing power they hold. The times we have shared with the people we love are extra precious to us and, as the hymn celebrates, memories of those times can give our "days gone by" a sacred feeling. Some of us are going through the process of saying goodbye to someone right now. Others may be facing the anniversary of a loved one's departure to their heavenly home. And still others find themselves sometimes overwhelmed out of the blue with feelings of missing a dear one greatly. This is something we're never alone in; we are surrounded by people who understand in their own way, because we've all been there at some point, and we will all be again.

There is something we can do in those moments—and remind others to do as well—and that's to draw close to God in prayer. Even simply sitting in His presence, allowing tears to flow and thanking Him for those memories He's blessed us with will help carry us through until we join the ones we love one day. In the meantime, let's pray that God would open our heart and mind to those forgotten things that can bring us comfort and peace. What a blessing it is when an image of the past comes to mind that we thought we'd completely forgotten. When someone we know is going through the sadness of loss, we can pray the same for them. "You have collected all my tears in Your bottle," David prays in Psalm 56:8 (NLT). He had experienced God's intimate love for His creation and knew that everything he was going through mattered deeply to Him. May that truth bring us comfort as we remember the precious scenes of our life.

Jesus, Your Word reminds us that even Your earthly mother
took time to store up her memories of You.
As I remember those who have gone before me, may those times
we have shared bring true comfort and peace to my heart.
And when those around me are experiencing the sadness of loss,
may they too find solace in all they have shared
with the ones they love.

AMEN.

THE ROCK THAT IS HIGHER THAN I

SEEK THE LORD AND HIS STRENGTH;
SEEK HIS PRESENCE CONTINUALLY!
PSALM 105:4 ESV

Sometimes (or many times!) in life, we reach a point where we're just tapped out. It could be the result of sleepless nights with a newborn, an overcommitted calendar, dealing with a health issue, facing a challenge that feels like it will never end . . . you get the idea. We're spent, exhausted, and just want to throw in the proverbial towel. But life keeps happening, the sun keeps rising, and we know we have to find our way through another day. When those times come, we can be certain that we're not alone. A significant part of our country's population reports too many days of too-little sleep. And it's not surprising. We don't experience the natural flow of life as much as our ancestors did. Their lives were attuned to the rhythm of the seasons; they rose and set with the sun. No 24-hour convenience stores, no late-night light shining on us from laptops and smart phones, no ability to try to be everywhere all at once. Sure, they had their own reasons for being tired (farm chores in the wee hours of the morning, anyone?), but things were surely simpler, and they were more present in their surroundings and circumstances because that's all they knew how to be.

Fast forward to the twenty-first century: We try to do it all, at all hours of the day and night. We give away our precious moments of rest in lots of ways—mindless TV, worrying about tomorrow's schedule the moment our head hits the pillow, trying to get one more thing checked off the to-do list (that is, unfortunately, still awaiting us in the morning!). It's no surprise that funny memes and T-shirts about caffeine abound because . . . we're tired and we want to fix it!

Know what we may need to do most in times like this? *Surrender.* Step away however we can. Find some quiet. Ask the Lord how we might experience His peace more deeply. What can we let go of? Who can we ask for help? How can we slow our pace—even if our circumstances are extra challenging right now? The words to the hymn "The Rock That Is Higher Than I" invite us to find rest in God's presence:

> *O sometimes how long seems the day,*
> *And sometimes how weary my feet;*
> *But toiling in life's dusty way,*
> *The Rock's blessed shadow, how sweet!*

When we feel as if we can't hold everything up anymore, we can remember that wasn't our job in the first place. Then we can lay it all down and offer it to Him. That's what we were designed to do anyway. The more of our own agenda we let go of, the more freedom we have to follow His lead. The more we seek His presence in our daily lives, the more peace we will experience in the midst of it all. As the Bible reminds us in Ephesians 2:14 (NIV), "He Himself is our peace." Nothing is more satisfying than a life lived in Christ, but it's something we have to choose day by day. Give yourself the gift of a few moments now and then, find a quiet place, and rest in that truth.

Jesus, thank You for being my Rock,
the One I can lean on through everything.
I know that the most joyful, peaceful life I can imagine
will be lived with that awareness.
When I'm stressed, overcommitted, or just plain exhausted,
help me to lay it all down and rest in You again.

AMEN.

THE ROCK THAT IS HIGHER THAN I

O sometimes the shadows are deep,
And rough seems the path to the goal;
And sorrows, sometimes how they sweep
Like tempests down over the soul!

O then to the Rock let me fly,
To the Rock that is higher than I;
O then to the Rock let me fly,
To the Rock that is higher than I!

O sometimes how long seems the day,
And sometimes how weary my feet;
But toiling in life's dusty way,
The Rock's blessed shadow, how sweet!

O near to the Rock let me keep,
If blessings or sorrow prevail;
Or climbing the mountainway steep,
Or walking the shadowy vale.

WE GIVE THEE
BUT THINE OWN

THEREFORE WELCOME ONE ANOTHER
AS CHRIST HAS WELCOMED YOU,
FOR THE GLORY OF GOD.
ROMANS 15:7 ESV

Being the new kid—it's not for the faint of heart. You may have had that experience growing up—moving to a new town, starting a new school, playing a new sport, joining a new club . . . anywhere a circle had already been formed that caused you to wonder whether someone would scoot over and offer you a spot beside them. As a child, it can be so important to find a place to fit. Enduring awkward stares, hidden whispers, and flat-out rejection can be devastating to young hearts. And a few decades down the road of our lives? It can *still* hurt like that when we feel left out. Adults may act differently, but in some ways, we're still all ten-year-olds inside, just dressed like grown-ups. We still feel that nervousness about being the "new person" in a job or an organization, church, or community. We still look for ways to fit in and long to be accepted for who we are. We still hope for that person who will step back to widen the circle and say, "Hey, here's a spot. What's your name?" That person—the one who keeps her eyes peeled for the "new kid"—reaches out to the struggling stranger or opens her heart to someone who has faced a lot of closed doors, and that person is living the truth of Matthew 25:40, whether she knows it or not: "Whatever you did for one of the least of these brothers and sisters of Mine, you did for Me" (NIV). We have the opportunity to be that person every day. The hymn "We Give Thee but Thine Own" is a lovely reminder that everything we do, we can choose to do for the Lord. After all, He has provided all we have—our time, our abilities, our possessions, our very lives—and we can offer Him those things in return, through acts of love toward those around us:

> *To comfort and to bless,*
> *To find a balm for woe,*
> *To tend the lone and fatherless*
> *Is angels' work below.*

Remember: as our lives ebb and flow, we will have plenty of opportunities to reach out, but we will also be the ones on the receiving end now and then. When you're the one entering a new situation, look for the open hearts nearby. Pray for God's presence to assure you and His guidance to help you find your place. Like any loving father, He wants you to know that you're loved and accepted just as you are. He can provide ways for you to feel the truth of that during times of transition. And when the tables are turned, always consider being the one who widens the circle. Be aware of new faces and take that simple step of offering a warm hello. And one final thought: We can live that example for the children in our lives too. Remind them that Jesus calls us to look for the one who is left out and invite them in. Give them the opportunity to feel the wonderful feeling that comes from doing something for the One who has given us everything.

Lord, may I always remember to look for those
who need a warm smile, a helping hand, or an open heart.
I know it blesses You when I share Your love,
especially with those who feel left out.
And when I'm the new kid, I thank You for the ways You show
Your love through those who reach out to me too.

AMEN.

HOW CAN I KEEP FROM SINGING?

TEACH ME YOUR WAY, LORD, THAT I MAY RELY ON YOUR FAITHFULNESS.
PSALM 86:11 NIV

"How Can I Keep from Singing" is a beautiful hymn about the vibrant life we're invited to live in Christ. It paints a picture of the peace and joy He brings against the backdrop of the world that can feel a little dark and heavy sometimes. It reminds us that the more we hold on to Him, the more our lives will flow with the quiet confidence that He is leading us through it all. Think for a moment of the times you have felt pressure to make a big decision, and remember how heavy it can feel when there's a lot riding on your next move. Now imagine that burden being lifted by the One who knows you intimately and has already laid the path ahead of you:

> *I lift my eyes; the cloud grows thin;*
> *I see the blue above it;*
> *And day by day this pathway smoothes,*
> *Since first I learned to love it.*

There's a big difference between surviving the journey and truly thriving in life, and it has much to do with who we're listening to for our ultimate guidance: the God within us or the world around us. People have their own ways of sharing opinions about what we're up to in our lives, especially when they don't understand why we're doing what we're doing. Have you noticed that? Depending on their personality, it can be a bold "What in the world are you thinking?!" or a more subtle "Hmm, that's an interesting idea." Just because that loving parent or dear friend of ours wouldn't consider packing up and moving, taking that job, going through with an adoption, traveling halfway across the world for whatever reason . . . that doesn't mean it's not right for us.

Of course, it will always serve us to be open to the wisdom and loving counsel of those who know us well, love us deeply, and want the very best for us in life. When we have people in our corner who care enough to share their concerns (whether we agree or not), that's a true gift! Not everyone has the courage to "speak the truth in love," and we should certainly cherish those who do. But in the end, *we* are the ones who will choose what step we take next in life. Times of change and transition can be challenging as we discern those big decisions that will affect not only our life, but the family and friends who are close to our heart. If we find ourselves feeling a little confused, pulled in more than one direction, or fearful about making the wrong choice, we can always remember that Jesus is already making a way. He is ready and willing to guide us, speaking to our heart in ways we may not even be aware of. No decision is too big or small to bring to Him. We can't surprise Him or baffle Him with our next step. And we can always say, "Lord, if I'm about to walk through the wrong door, slam it shut!" With that confidence, we can prayerfully take the step we feel most led to. And even if the path isn't as smooth as we expected, our heart can rest assured that He will see us through.

Lord, I don't want to dread the decisions in my life.
When it's time to make a choice,
I want to remember that You are always there
to lighten my load, guiding me by Your Spirit
and supporting me through the wisdom of loved ones who care.
Whatever I choose, may it be for my highest good
and Your glory.

AMEN.

FIGHT THE GOOD FIGHT

BUT WE HAVE THE MIND OF CHRIST.
I CORINTHIANS 2:16 KJV

"Get out of your own way": We hear that phrase a lot, but what does it mean? How is it possible to get out of our own way? Are those words actually helpful to a person who feels stuck and needs some encouragement? Well, someone who gives us that advice has likely noticed that we've limited ourselves in some way. They may have seen us shying away from a step we are perfectly capable of taking, or they believe we have all we need to do what we're dreaming of, but see that we're allowing our thoughts to hold us back. Our mind can do a fantastic job of convincing us that we can't do something *and* providing a long and detailed list of exactly why that is. Then there are the fears that creep in: What if I didn't hear God correctly? What if I take a step in one direction and realize that it's not my path after all? What will happen if I try but *fail*?

Many of us have felt these feelings, and we're never alone in them. But what we sometimes forget is that *we* are not the only ones in our way; there's an enemy of our soul who endeavors to block our path too. An enemy who lives to steal our joy and convince us that we have no chance, no ability, and no worth. If we take a prayerful step toward something we believe God has in store for us, we can be certain that there will be a counter move from the enemy. No matter what measure of "success" we achieve, the mere fact that we're drawing close to our Maker is a direct hit on the darkness. The things we endeavor to do in our lives, whatever they may be, are about so much more than a destination. They're about learning to walk in the light regardless of what we're doing, and that means seeking God's guidance and His presence above all and also listening to the voice of the Spirit over any other voice that competes for our attention (including our own fearful self-talk!). Having the "mind of

Christ" (I Corinthians 2:16) is the single greatest protection we have from getting in our own way—or allowing anyone else to! The more we absorb the truths from His Word about who we are in Him, the less room there will be for doubt and negativity to creep in. We can move forward with more freedom and less fear, more joy and less stress, more trust that everything is unfolding just as He intends. The hymn "Fight the Good Fight" has encouraged believers through the years to find our strength and confidence in Christ alone:

> *Run the straight race through God's good grace,*
> *Lift up thine eyes, and seek His face;*
> *Life with its way before us lies,*
> *Christ is the path, and Christ the prize.*

Paul's reminder in Romans 12:2 (NIV) to "be transformed by the renewing of your mind" is vital for us in a world that will offer countless other ideas of how to "get out of our own way." There is only One who knows exactly what we're up to and why; only One who deeply understands our doubts and fears and offers all we need to clear the path ahead. Instead of keeping that narrow focus on whatever we're trying to accomplish, we're invited to keep our eyes on Him and enjoy the journey. There's nothing on earth we could earn or achieve that brings the amount of satisfaction we find through walking with Jesus.

Dear God, sometimes my thoughts stand in the way
of enjoying and experiencing all You have for me in my life.
When I sense that struggle in my mind,
I want to remember that You have given me the mind of Christ.
May every fearful, anxious, or negative thought that comes up
be replaced by Your promises of peace and assurance.

AMEN.

I LOVE TO TELL THE STORY

ONE GENERATION SHALL
COMMEND YOUR WORKS TO ANOTHER,
AND SHALL DECLARE YOUR MIGHTY ACTS.
PSALM 145:4 ESV

Storytelling has been around for as long as we humans have. From the beginning of creation, we have used storytelling in one form or another to connect, to make sense of our lives and the world around us, and to pass along those things we feel matter most. When we open our Bible and see the words printed on paper, we should remember that they weren't always written down to read. At one point it was all word of mouth—one person doing their best to tell another about the profound things that had happened, both within and around them. We can only imagine what it was like for people to try to express their encounters with God, the miracles they witnessed, the struggles they endured, and the hope they held that their heavenly Father would fulfill His promises as He'd said. We are no more human than those storytellers were in their time. And just as they did, we feel the need to share our stories in our own ways. One day the stories of our lives will be left behind like fingerprints for those who come after us. They'll be shared among our loved ones, proof that we once walked through this world and left our mark. As Christ followers, the most significant and powerful part of our stories will be about who He is to us. Once we come to know Him, our legacy changes; it's not just about leaving our own wisdom and experience behind. It's about leaving a trail for other hearts to meet Him for themselves and be forever changed like we were. The hymn "I Love to Tell the Story" shares the joy that comes when we have that opportunity:

I love to tell the story;
'Twill be my theme in glory—
To tell the old, old story
Of Jesus and His love.

As the years pass, we think more often about the kind of legacies we'll leave. What are our lives telling the next generation right now? And what will they remember about us when we're gone? We might have an aging parent or grandparent who brings this to our attention as they share accounts of their own lives. We cherish those memories, and sometimes we record or write them down to keep as treasures. When someone we love faces a serious illness or there's an unexpected death close to us, we are quickly reminded that we're not promised tomorrow. Regardless of how many days we're given on this earth, we do have this day to cherish right now. This is the day for living our stories. This is the day for seeking God's presence in our lives; maybe one day we'll be inspired to tell someone else about our experience. The stories we share not only build the faith of others but also remind us of who we are and whose we are. We won't always find the words to describe our journeys through this life, but when we do, may they point many others to the One who lives through us.

Lord, may my words and actions always tell Your story
in some way. I know that my legacy is no longer my own;
it is Yours because I belong to You. I want my life to reflect
Your grace, mercy, goodness, power, healing, strength,
and love in countless ways. Even when I am gone
from this world, may my story inspire others
to surrender their lives to You.

AMEN.

SPIRIT HOLY

BUT THE FRUIT OF THE SPIRIT IS LOVE, JOY,
PEACE, FORBEARANCE, KINDNESS, GOODNESS,
FAITHFULNESS, GENTLENESS AND SELF-CONTROL.
AGAINST SUCH THINGS THERE IS NO LAW.
GALATIANS 5:22–23 NIV

Do you happen to know one of those people (or maybe it's you!) who is a natural chef? They may start with a recipe, but they know just how to add in an extra pinch of this or a teaspoon of that to make it better. They look at those ingredients and measurements as great suggestions but then decide to run with it. By the time the finished product is in the oven, they may have created a whole new dish. For those of us whose personalities are more go-with-the-flow, this makes perfect sense. Of *course* we can figure it out as we go along, do our own thing, and see what we discover along the way. That's all part of the fun! But for others, the idea of deviating from that recipe is daunting. We're rule followers. We like structure. If it says a cup, we put in a cup! What else would you do? And guess what? That casserole comes out tasting exactly as it's supposed to. It's a no-brainer, right? So which chef is doing it correctly? The one who brings her creativity to the kitchen and looks for new ways to delight the taste buds? Or the one whose attention to detail is unmatched and can be counted on for a consistent presentation every time? Well . . . *both*! It's all about the outcome. Did they each end up with something wonderful? Yes! And the proof . . . as they say . . . is in the pudding.

As you might guess, there's a life lesson for us here. When we are facing times of change, we may think we have a pretty solid recipe for making it through. We've formed an idea of what it will be like—perhaps based on the experience of others or what we ourselves have weathered in the past. Maybe when our neighbor went through it, her experience looked like such-and-such. Or when that friend of ours tried something similar, *this* is what happened to him. The last time we faced that sort of thing, we had *this* particular outcome. We make assumptions about how it's going to play out before we've even tasted the experience. But living by the Spirit doesn't have to be like that. It's not about whether we're sticking to a "recipe"—it's a whole different way of looking at life. The more we follow His lead, the less we worry about what it's "supposed" to be like. We can be more "in the moment," resting in the knowledge that He is always up to something good in our lives. As the hymn "Spirit Holy" expresses:

Spirit holy in me dwelling,
Ever work as Thou shalt choose;
All my ransomed pow'rs and talents
For Thy purpose Thou shalt use.

There are many ways to experience times of change, and our personalities certainly play a role in how we approach them. But we can all benefit from listening closely to the Spirit to guide us through. What will our lives look like when we come out on the other side? Only God knows, but His Word reminds us that the more of His presence we enjoy in the process, the more love, joy, peace, patience, kindness, goodness, faithfulness, gentleness, and self-control we will possess. Those are the ingredients of a beautiful life, and no matter what we face, they are always available to us in Him.

Holy Spirit, Yours is the only voice I need to guide me
through this life. It's such a relief to rest in that truth.
Instead of trying to control it all, I want to bring everything
to You. I know that the journey with You is so much
more important than whatever I think I'm accomplishing.
Help me to become a little more like You each day.

AMEN.

O SPIRIT OF THE LIVING GOD

*DEATH AND LIFE ARE
IN THE POWER OF THE TONGUE.
PROVERBS 18:21 KJV*

The hymn "O Spirit of the Living God" is like a prayer sung to the Holy Spirit, calling on Him to fill us, heal us, and make us all one in Christ:

> *Give tongues of fire and hearts of love*
> *To preach the reconciling word;*
> *Anoint with power from heaven above*
> *Whenever gospel truth is heard.*

As the song reveals, one way we share His love is through our words. And as most of us have learned in life, the words we speak matter more than we sometimes realize. Even if we don't fully understand how it all works, God has fashioned this magnificent universe in such a way that what we say can have great power. Clearly, what *He* says has the greatest and most awe-inspiring power of all. When He spoke life into existence, He created something from nothing and sustains it for all eternity. The Bible reminds us that when we look at Christ, we see the truth of that: "The Son is the radiance of God's glory and the exact representation of His being, sustaining all things by His powerful Word" (Hebrews 1:3 NIV). We hear Jesus called "the Word made flesh" and "the Living Word"— titles that reflect the absolute purity and integrity of His incarnation. He was (and is) the perfect expression of the Father, speaking His love to the world in a way our hearts can receive and understand.

As we think about how we might follow Him more closely, let's reflect on the words that come from our mouth. How often do our words encourage and uplift . . . and how often do they criticize and tear down? Are there times we could give someone grace by remaining quiet even though we feel they really "deserve" a piece of our mind? Are there opportunities we can take to speak life to another who truly needs it right then? Here's something to consider: If we were to draw a comic strip of our lives, would those word bubbles be filled with more goodness than grumbling? In our most challenging times, our words will be extra revealing because we tend to lose our filter in survival mode. Those are the times we catch ourselves saying things we don't mean and hurting others in ways we would never intend. If we want to keep speaking words of life, regardless of our circumstances, we would be wise to store up those kinds of words in our heart today. And, of course, the ultimate place to find words of life is in God's Word itself. The more we fill up with His promises and focus on all we can be grateful for, the more goodness will spill out of our mouth and into our life no matter what we're facing. As the hymn reminds us, His love is a language that all can understand, and we can speak that language fluently if we choose.

Heavenly Father, I know that the words I choose
truly make a difference, even if I sometimes forget that.
Help me to fill my heart with Your promises
so that when I encounter life's challenges,
Your words of love and truth will be on my lips.
Thank You for all the ways You provide for us
to live this life in peace and joy.

AMEN.

DEAR LORD AND FATHER OF MANKIND

NOW MAY THE LORD OF PEACE HIMSELF
GIVE YOU PEACE AT ALL TIMES AND IN EVERY WAY.
II THESSALONIANS 3:16 NIV

When it comes to preparing for things, we all have mental lists. Athletes know just what gear they'll take along for every game; moms going on playdates could pack those diaper bags in their sleep (and sometimes do!); and most of us have all our grocery-store necessities memorized because . . . weren't we just there yesterday? Sure, there may be some things on those lists that fluctuate, but others are nonnegotiable: the helmet, the diaper, the butter—you know, those essentials we just can't imagine being without. If you think about it, we have a spiritual list like that, too, whether or not we are conscious of it. We know the essentials we need to carry within us wherever we go, and one of the biggies for many of us is God's peace. It's especially important when we are entering unfamiliar territory in our lives. New opportunities and challenges, new faces and places, new seasons of growth and change—these are times when His peace is truly a necessity. The hymn "Dear Lord and Father of Mankind" is like a prayer for times like those that call us back to the simplicity of silence where we hear the still, small voice of the Spirit:

> Take from our souls the strain and stress,
> And let our ordered lives confess
> The beauty of Thy peace.

What do our lives confess today? When others look at us, do they see the peace of Christ or the chaos of the world? Obviously, we're all going to have meltdowns, stressful times, and less-than-ideal reactions from time to time. Most of us are juggling a lot these days, and it can be hard to find that calm center. But the peace of God is a deeper thing people witness in us. It's an assurance that even though the road is rough in the moment, all will be well in the end. It's that surrendered prayer at the end of the day that says, "Lord, I did my best; it was far from perfect, but I'm so grateful that You love me just the same." It's the conviction that nothing we say or do can ever steal what has been given us through Christ. As we learn to walk in His peace, our lives become less stressful and more satisfying. And not only that, but others will see His reflection in us and be drawn to it. Think of a body of water on a windy day: the constant waves make it impossible to see a clear image reflected. But when that water is still, the reflection can be beautiful. Even if we feel fearful, nervous, or unsure about what we're facing in life, let's remember the wisdom of this hymn. The peace we carry within us is always accessible and infinitely greater than anything going on outside us. And the more we live from that place of assurance, the more our lives will reflect our Savior's love.

Jesus, I want to carry Your peace within me wherever I go.
When I'm entering unfamiliar territory in my life,
remind me to return to that calm center where Your Spirit
awaits to quiet my heart. When others look at me,
even in my humanness, may they somehow see You
and be drawn to the quiet assurance
of Your constant presence.

AMEN.

O THE DEEP, DEEP LOVE OF JESUS

AND I PRAY THAT YOU,
BEING ROOTED AND ESTABLISHED IN LOVE,
MAY HAVE POWER, TOGETHER
WITH ALL THE LORD'S HOLY PEOPLE,
TO GRASP HOW WIDE AND LONG AND HIGH
AND DEEP IS THE LOVE OF CHRIST.
EPHESIANS 3:17-18 NIV

How do you feel about being alone? That's a big question that can mean a lot of things. If you're an introvert, the word "alone" may not feel too scary. In fact, it may sound quite appealing after a long day of too much "peopling." An extrovert, on the other hand, might not be terribly fond of the idea. For some of us, "alone" is a time that can be used for refreshing and recharging. For others, it can be a time when we feel more anxiety and restlessness. Regardless, spending a little time by ourselves is one thing, but going through a transition that takes people out of our lives is another. Those transitions can be tough no matter what kind of personality we have. Regardless of whether we like being around a lot of people, there are special ones who are such a big part of life that we can't imagine being without them. How do we navigate the changes that take our people away temporarily or permanently in the difficult end of a significant relationship, the first year of an empty nest, a best friend moving far away, or the loss of a loved one who was dear to us? Those are the times when we need to feel the love of Jesus deeply. We need to be aware of His very real presence with us and know that we are never the only one in a room: He is always there. "O the Deep, Deep Love of Jesus" comforts the heart with this truth:

Underneath me, all around me,
Is the current of Thy love
Leading onward, leading homeward,
To Thy glorious rest above.

Having this anchor in times of change makes all the difference in the world. No, it doesn't stop us from having to feel the hard stuff, but it does give us Someone to hold on to through it all. If we suddenly find ourselves with more alone time than we like, we can use some of that time to prayerfully process our difficult experiences. Maybe we can journal about what we're going through, capture some memories, or reflect on God's promises concerning times of change and even loneliness, if that's what we're feeling. Those seasons of life often open up more space for us to redirect our energy. What about creating lists of things we've been wanting to try, people to reach out to, or places to see? If we're missing a particular person, what about surprising them by sending a handwritten note? (Who takes time to do that anymore?) And if that person we're missing has gone home to be with Jesus, we can write that note anyway, say the things our heart needs to say, and tuck it away in a special place. That alone can be a healing experience. No matter how we move through times of change, let us never forget that "in Him we live and move and have our being" (Acts 17:28 NIV). That's something we can count on for eternity.

Lord Jesus, You're my constant companion,
and I'm so grateful for that. Change can be unsettling for me,
especially when it involves the people I love.
Knowing that You are with me through it all means everything.
When I feel alone, help me see the ways I can use my time
and energy for good. Thank You for Your never-ending love.

AMEN.

NEARER, MY GOD, TO THEE

"AM I NOT EVERYWHERE IN ALL THE HEAVENS
AND EARTH?" SAYS THE LORD.
JEREMIAH 23:24 NLT

Perhaps there is no greater gift during times of change than God's unchanging presence. No matter where we are or what we're up to, that Presence is the one thing we can be 100 percent certain of. Sometimes we forget to pay attention, though. We might have a habit of mentally separating life into the sacred and the secular. Our days may be filled with business-as-usual, mundane tasks—nothing that "feels" very spiritual or inspires our awe in any way. But when we switch gears and enter that quiet space we've set aside for prayer or take a seat in church or meet up with our small group with the intent of digging into deeper things, we tend to turn our thoughts toward Him more easily. That's a wonderful thing! But it also means there can be a pretty big part of life outside the "spiritual bubble," when we're not doing the things that feel more sacred. Know that He delights in making Himself known to us in the everydayness of our lives too.

Think of Moses encountering the burning bush while tending sheep on Mount Horeb (not a very sacred-sounding activity!). God tells him, "Take off your sandals, for the place where you are standing is holy ground" (Exodus 3:5 NIV). God calls that spot where Moses is already standing "holy." Not another cleaner, more spiritual destination, but *that one*. Recall the words of Jacob as he awakens from that dream where the Lord appears to him at the top of a ladder in the middle of nowhere: "Surely the LORD is in this place, and I was not aware of it." And then his realization, "How awesome is this place! This is none other than the house of God; this is the gate of heaven" (Genesis 28:16–17 NIV). His location did not change; he just became aware of God's presence right where he was. The hymn "Nearer, My God, to Thee" speaks of Jacob's story—and of our desire as God's children to be near to Him in every way:

> *There let the way appear, steps unto heaven;*
> *All that Thou sendest me, in mercy given;*
> *Angels to beckon me*
> *Nearer, my God, to Thee.*

So how do we make that happen? How do we experience more of God wherever we are? We know it's not about trying harder, being holier, or finding the right formula. It *is* about our awareness. There may not be many burning bushes or angelic ladders to capture our attention, but we can practice being more open to His presence in our own way. Maybe we commit to a walk around the block each day with the sole purpose of enjoying His company in nature. Maybe we place some touchstones in everyday spaces that remind us to turn our heart toward Him for a moment as we pass by. As we become more aware of His presence in our day-to-day life, we will be more prepared for those times when we truly need to know that He is with us during every moment.

> *Lord, I want to experience Your presence everywhere.*
> *How awesome to know that there's no place I will ever go*
> *and nothing I will ever go through without You.*
> *How can I remind myself of this every day?*
> *Thank You for being an intimate God*
> *who wants to share all my moments with me.*

AMEN.

NEARER, MY GOD, TO THEE

Nearer, my God, to Thee, nearer to Thee!
E'en though it be a cross that raiseth me,
Still all my song shall be,
Nearer, my God, to Thee;
Nearer, my God, to Thee, nearer to Thee!

Though like the wanderer, the sun gone down,
Darkness be over me, my rest a stone;
Yet in my dreams I'd be
Nearer, my God, to Thee;
Nearer, my God, to Thee, nearer to Thee!

There let the way appear, steps unto heaven;
All that Thou sendest me, in mercy given;
Angels to beckon me
Nearer, my God, to Thee;
Nearer, my God, to Thee, nearer to Thee!

Then, with my waking thoughts bright with
    Thy praise,
Out of my stony griefs Bethel I'll raise;
So by my woes to be
Nearer, my God, to Thee;
Nearer, my God, to Thee, nearer to Thee!

Or if, on joyful wing cleaving the sky,
Sun, moon, and stars forgot, upward I fly,
Still all my song shall be,
Nearer, my God, to Thee;
Nearer, my God, to Thee, nearer to Thee!

THE STRIFE IS O'ER, THE BATTLE DONE

WHEN I AM AFRAID, I PUT MY TRUST IN YOU.
PSALM 56:3 NIV

If we're honest, we all have things we've wanted to do, or even felt called to do, but turned back out of fear. Fear of harm. Fear of failure. Fear of what others might think. Fear of the unknown. Fear is one of those things we will never escape in this life because it's part of the brokenness of the world we live in. But let us never forget that we don't have to be controlled by it. Fear is not allowed to make our choices for us or to stop us from trying something new or to prevent us from moving toward whatever God is calling us to. Fear is like rain; we can stand in it and allow it to drench us, or we can put up those umbrellas and stay dry beneath them. The rain does not disappear when the umbrella goes up; it just doesn't touch us anymore. In the same way, those feelings of fear will continue to show up, but they don't have to sway our decisions or ruin our experience. We can live with courage and confidence in the face of them. How? Under the covering of our Savior's love.

His love is there in every moment of every situation for every person who would put their trust in Him. Even when we forget who He is for us, He remembers. Even when we hesitate to step out, He beckons us boldly. And even when we begin to panic like Peter as the wind and the waves rise, He offers us His hand of assurance. There is nothing we will try that He will not walk through with us. If that means making a U-turn once in a while, that's okay! Whatever we endeavor, we do the best we can with the wisdom we have at the time. We step forward in confidence, knowing that nothing will happen that's not already in His hands. All the "what-ifs" in the world can't touch our unwavering trust in Him. And if we really want to look fear in the face, we can ask ourselves, "What's the worst thing that can happen in this situation?" What we answer probably won't happen, but at least we're not afraid to put it out there. There's something freeing about knowing that even the worst thing we can imagine would be covered by His love. Jesus has already met the worst for us and conquered it. We already know the end. Until then, we're invited to a life of joy and purpose; we are offered a freedom that we sometimes forget the magnitude of—freedom from saving ourselves in every way. It has already been done on our behalf. That is the message of the victorious hymn "The Strife is O'er, the Battle Done":

The powers of death have done their worst,
But Christ their legions has dispersed;
Let shouts of holy joy outburst.
Alleluia!

It has been said that because of Christ, the worst thing will never be the last thing. What a wonderful truth to remember. We may go through tough times of doubt and uncertainty, but the destination we're heading toward will far outshine anything we've gone through to get there.

Lord Jesus, because of You,
I will never have to be controlled by fear.
I am free to make decisions, to live with courage and
confidence, and to fulfill Your purposes for me in this life,
all because You have made a way.
Thank You for enduring the worst so that I could know
God's best for me today and throughout eternity.

AMEN.

THE OLD RUGGED CROSS

THEN JESUS SAID TO HIS DISCIPLES,
"IF ANY OF YOU WANTS TO BE MY FOLLOWER,
YOU MUST GIVE UP YOUR OWN WAY,
TAKE UP YOUR CROSS, AND FOLLOW ME."
MATTHEW 16:24 NLT

When the hymn "The Old Rugged Cross" begins to play, many of us recognize it immediately. It's one of those songs sung through the generations, pointing us to the symbol of our salvation and all it means to us:

So I'll cherish the old rugged cross,
Till my trophies at last I lay down;
I will cling to the old rugged cross
And exchange it some day for a crown.

One definition of *cherish* is "to keep or cultivate with care and affection." When we speak of cherishing the cross, we are expressing how deeply we treasure the sacrifice Christ made for us. The sight of that symbol can fill us with a sense of love and gratitude unlike any other. But it also invites us to follow in His footsteps. As the definition suggests, we can show that we cherish something by cultivating it. That means we don't just have sentimental feelings about the cross; instead, we feel compelled to live the truth of it out in the world today. But what does that look like? Among other things, it looks like sacrifice, surrender, and Spirit-led living. It looks like letting go of our own agendas so that we can embrace what God has for us instead. And we can always trust that what He has for us will be more nurturing to our spirit and satisfying to our soul than anything we could come up with, no matter how enticing our own ideas may seem. He will never ask us to carry something He has not prepared us for. As Jesus reminds us in Matthew 11:30, "My yoke is easy and my burden is light" (NIV). We need to remember this, especially when our times of change include a sacrifice of some kind. There will be paths in life that we would not have taken without the nudge of the Spirit. And those paths may not look like the "easy" way at all . . . in fact, they may look downright difficult. They may involve laying something down that's precious to us or putting someone else's needs before our own, for a time or permanently. There may be some kind of thankless volunteer work we're called to or being the one to take that first humbling step toward the repair of a relationship.

Our lifetime will bring many opportunities to "take up the cross" as we share the love of Jesus in very real and tangible ways. We are bound to go through times of feeling frustrated, uncomfortable, or discouraged because we're human, and as much as we want to be part of bringing His kingdom to earth, we know the journey is not always going to be full of roses. When we feel like throwing in the towel, we can always return to the image of our Savior giving it all for us. What we do in return is never about earning His love or proving ourselves; it's about cherishing Him and those He created and called His own. Remembering who we're living for will make those times of sacrifice so much sweeter. And when we look at that old rugged cross, we will know that we have had a little part in helping someone else to experience the eternal love it represents.

Jesus, You gave Your all for us,
and I want to give all I can to You. How are You calling me
to set aside my comfort and agenda so that
Your sacrificial love will shine through in my life?
Every time I look at the cross, may I remember the priceless gift
I received and be inspired to share it in every way I can.

AMEN.

SOVEREIGN RULER
OF THE SKIES

YET WHO KNOWS WHETHER YOU HAVE COME
TO THE KINGDOM FOR SUCH A TIME AS THIS?
ESTHER 4:14 NKJV

"Time will tell." "Turn back time." "All in good time." We have countless sayings about time because it affects pretty much everything we do. It was part of this universe long before we arrived on the scene, and it'll be here as long as our Maker says so. Our experience of time can feel a little like being on a train that we didn't buy a ticket for, but it's barreling ahead and we're along for the ride whether we like it or not. Minutes turn to hours . . . to days . . . to months . . . to years and there's nothing we can do to slow it down or stop it. It's a bittersweet feeling as we grow older, and we increasingly learn to savor our moments because we know there will only be so many of them. However, knowing that this earth is not our final destination changes everything. We can rejoice in the fact that eternity awaits and we're all just passing through. But while we're here, this thing called "time" is part of our story and God has made it very clear that it has great purpose in our life. We all have moments when we get a sense that the time is right for something. Maybe something has shifted or come to fruition or we're suddenly feeling the nudge to pay careful attention to how our journey is unfolding. It's good to tune into that nudge; it is very possible that our Creator is revealing something to us that is meant for this very moment. As the well-known message of Ecclesiastes 3:1 reminds us: "There is a time for everything, and a season for every activity under the heavens" (NIV). We don't live in a chaotic, disordered universe (even if it seems that way!). We can trust that there is order and intention behind everything God allows, and we have a purposeful part in it all. The hymn "Sovereign Ruler of the Skies" celebrates that wonderful Providence who can bring us great comfort and assurance in the face of life's uncertainties:

> *Sovereign Ruler of the skies,*
> *Ever gracious, ever wise!*
> *All our times are in Thy hand,*
> *All events at Thy command.*

When we have the sense that the time has arrived for some kind of change, we can ask the Lord to help us understand it more clearly. It could be some healing from our past that was just not possible until that moment. It might be a dream that's been on the back burner of our heart for years and suddenly things are lining up to make it happen. It could be someone we've been meaning to reach out to and, for whatever reason, we sense the Spirit saying, "Now." The more open we are to God's timing, the less we fret about trying to control things or make them happen our own way. It's no accident that we're here "for such a time as this," and one day maybe we will have the privilege of seeing how it all wove together so intricately.

> *Creator God, time is a fascinating thing and,*
> *just like all You have made,*
> *it serves a great purpose in Your kingdom.*
> *Help me to let go and trust that all my hours, days,*
> *and years are covered by Your sovereign hand.*
> *May I hear Your voice clearly when the moment arrives*
> *for something significant in my life.*
>
> ## AMEN.

COME, THOU LONG EXPECTED JESUS

LET ALL THAT I AM WAIT QUIETLY BEFORE GOD,
FOR MY HOPE IS IN HIM.
PSALM 62:5 NLT

The hymn "Come, Thou Long Expected Jesus" reflects the longing we all have for the day we see Him face-to-face. It speaks of release, freedom, and deliverance—all things we don't have to wait to experience until the end of our earthly life. We can receive those things in our own way, every day. It all depends on . . . well, *who* we're depending on! The Bible has a lot to say about where we pin our hopes; if we're waiting for something or someone other than Christ to bring our ultimate fulfillment, it's a sure path to disappointment. As the hymn reminds us, He is all we will ever need:

Israel's strength and consolation,
Hope of all the earth Thou art;
Dear desire of every nation,
Joy of every longing heart.

When we're planning to do something new and different, it's very likely that we will have some expectations attached. That's just how we're wired. The capacity for expectation is a wonderful gift! It's like one of our spiritual muscles. How else could we hope for things? How could we trust that God's promises will come to fruition, even before we see the evidence? Expectation is as any gift we've been given—it's our choice how to use it. Without realizing it, some of us become very attached to particular outcomes. We know exactly how we're hoping something will play out, and when it does, that's wonderful! But when it doesn't, it may take a while for us to move past our disappointment. Other people are more "go-with-the-flow." If it happens, great! If it doesn't, it just wasn't meant to be. It's like the difference between using superglue and tape: Superglue is tough to remove once you've committed to it. (Ever gotten your fingers stuck together with that stuff?) Tape, on the other hand, sticks when you need it, but it's not permanent.

In the same way, the more time and energy we spend while attaching ourselves to certain outcomes, the more effort it will take to free ourselves from the disappointment that can follow if it doesn't work out as we'd hoped. We can begin to loosen our grip on those expectations as we deepen our trust in the One who holds the outcome in His hands. Whether or not we want to admit it, we have no idea how that new endeavor or experience we're walking into will go down. We can always hope for the best, and God's Word reminds us that hoping and believing are vital for us in any situation! *But . . .* our faith is not in our expectations; ultimately, our faith is in our Provider. He will never disappoint us or leave us hanging. He may show up in ways we hadn't thought possible. He may open doors we didn't even know existed. He may even allow us to experience a few "losses" in order to remind us where our true treasure lies. No matter what we're walking into, let's draw close to Him for assurance. When expectations arise, let's bring them to Him. And let's live in the freedom that comes with letting go of our agenda and receiving everything He has for us, which is always "immeasurably more than all we ask or imagine" (Ephesians 3:20 NIV).

Lord, I get attached to what I want to happen.
But You are the One who knows every detail of my life
and sees exactly how it unfolds. Help me place my hope
in You alone and to trust that everything else will work out
as You intend. Thank You for all You are to me.

AMEN.

A LITTLE HUMAN KINDNESS

*IN THE SAME WAY,
LET YOUR LIGHT SHINE BEFORE OTHERS,
THAT THEY MAY SEE YOUR GOOD DEEDS
AND GLORIFY YOUR FATHER IN HEAVEN.
MATTHEW 5:16 NIV*

It's a Wonderful Life is a beloved classic film from the 1940s about George Bailey, a man who has fallen on hard times. Such hard times, in fact, that he begins to wonder whether his life even matters at all. Through a series of events, George is allowed to see what the world would be like if he had never been born. As he reviews the timeline of his life, he is surprised to discover how many things he has done that have actually made a big difference in others' lives—like choosing to do the right thing, regardless of the consequences. Like being generous without expecting a reward. Or showing grace when others would not and bringing joy to his family and friends in his special way. He witnesses the ripple effect of his own actions and also what may have happened to people had he not been in their lives during significant moments. The moral of the story: *every person matters infinitely, whether they realize it or not.* "A Little Human Kindness" is a little-known hymn that celebrates those ways we help bring God's kingdom to earth for others:

> *By making someone happy*
> *As we pass along life's way,*
> *We bring a bit of heaven*
> *To the longest, darkest day.*

We can learn a lot from that simple but powerful message. There will likely be seasons in our lives when we feel a little insignificant—maybe unappreciated, undervalued, or, let's be honest, just plain invisible. There will be times when life has shifted us out of the spotlight and into the wings, away from the front lines and into a place where we're living largely behind the scenes. We could be experiencing a shift in our role at work or the changing needs within our family—or perhaps something we do quietly so that someone else can shine. Maybe it's many years of loving on little ones in everyday ways and trusting that, even though they can't comprehend it now, what we are pouring into them will bless them throughout their lives.

It's wonderful to know that we're making a difference, even when we can't see it . . . but that doesn't make it easy! So what do we do when we're in the trenches? How can we be encouraged to "keep on keepin' on," regardless of whether we see the fruits of our labor during those moments? Well, for starters, we can look to God's Word for reminders that what we do for others matters eternally. We are called to "encourage one another" (I Thessalonians 5:11 NIV) and "bear one another's burdens" (Galatians 6:2 ESV). "Let us not become weary in doing good," Paul reminds us in Galatians 6:9, "for at the proper time we will reap a harvest if we do not give up" (NIV). When we're feeling less than significant, we can remind ourselves that no matter what role we're currently playing, every little kindness truly matters. Every word, smile, hug, offer of help, moment of listening, or gift of grace . . . whatever it is we feel led to do in the present is part of a much bigger picture that we will one day fully understand.

*Lord, those times when I feel unseen and unappreciated
are hard for me. When I feel discouraged and I'm hoping
that someone will notice how hard I'm trying, please remind me
that You see it all. You appreciate every detail and
You smile on me with love, and that is more than enough
for me to feel my worth, no matter what.*

AMEN.

ALL HAIL THE POWER OF JESUS'S NAME

BUT TO ALL WHO DID RECEIVE HIM,
WHO BELIEVED IN HIS NAME,
HE GAVE THE RIGHT TO BECOME CHILDREN OF GOD.
JOHN 1:12 ESV

Many songs have been written through the years about the name of Jesus, and for good reason! The Bible reminds us that at His name, "every knee shall bow" one day (Philippians 2:10 TLB). That's some power right there! Not a worldly kind of power that controls and overwhelms, but a power that stirs the heart of those who see Him for who He is . . . "the radiance of God's glory and the exact representation of His being" (Hebrews 1:3 NIV). The well-known hymn "All Hail the Power of Jesus's Name" celebrates that universal invitation to lift Him high in our hearts:

> *Let every kindred, every tribe,*
> *On this terrestrial ball,*
> *To Him all majesty ascribe,*
> *And crown Him Lord of all!*

So let's talk about names for a moment. If we grew up in the West, we've probably had a different experience with naming than people in Middle Eastern biblical times. Our parents may have selected our moniker from a baby name list or chosen it to honor a friend or family member. But when Jesus walked the earth, children's names had a lot more context. Sometimes they were a reflection of the child's anticipated mission in life or represented a spiritual vision or prophetic message. As the angel of the Lord said to Joseph in his dream, "You are to give Him the name Jesus, because He will save His people from their sins" (Matthew 1:21 NIV).

What does His name mean to us, then? Everything! And why is that so important to remember? Because sometimes we forget who we are in Him. The world does a fantastic job of helping us with that. Look at your license or passport and you'll see some things that are used to identify you as a citizen. Your physical appearance, address, date of birth—all factors that help distinguish you from the other seven and a half billion or so people in the world. Our identity can be a tricky thing because part of it is constantly transforming. Are you a mom? A daughter? A friend? A hard worker? A volunteer? A club member? Are you the funny one? The smart one? The one everyone comes to for advice? The hermit? The social butterfly? The trendsetter? We will be a lot of things in life, but none of them will define us forever. You might be a toddler mom now, but not too many years down the road, you'll watch that "baby" of yours drive off into his or her future. You might have a very meaningful job today, but someday that job will come to an end and you'll move on to your next endeavor. All the things you've been will remain a part of you, but none of them will ever define the whole of you. That definition is reserved for God alone, and in Christ, you are first and foremost His child. Your role may change a hundred times, but your true name will never change. How wonderful is that? It's one of those treasures we can hold on to, especially during transitions in life as we move from what we were to what we're becoming. We'll be grown, shaped, molded, transformed, renewed, reinvented . . . but we'll never lose the name we received when we became His. That's when our true life began, and because of who He is for us, we know that life will never end.

Jesus, Your name means everything to me. You are the reason for all that I am, all that I have, and all that I hope for. No matter what changes I may experience in this life, help me remember that my eternal identity will always be found in You.

AMEN.

I SING THE MIGHTY
POWER OF GOD

HAVE YOU NOT KNOWN?
HAVE YOU NOT HEARD?
THE LORD IS THE EVERLASTING GOD,
THE CREATOR OF THE ENDS OF THE EARTH.
HE DOES NOT FAINT OR GROW WEARY;
HIS UNDERSTANDING IS UNSEARCHABLE.
ISAIAH 40:28 ESV

Think about some of the first-time experiences you've had—opportunities you've taken, new relationships, home or career moves, steps of faith into uncharted territory. When it comes to opening unfamiliar doors, we all have a different approach. Some of us anticipate the unknown on the other side as if it were a new adventure, wondering what we might discover. Others draw near with more caution, hopeful but uncertain, imagining different scenarios that could play out. But most of us, if we're honest, have had at least a little anxiety at one time or another about stepping onto a new path. After all, we have no idea what's ahead. We may *think* we know. We may have others' experiences to draw from. Perhaps we made as many preparations as possible to eliminate all the X-factors we could think of. But in the end, this is something we've never done and (try as we might!) we have to admit that we aren't the ones running the show. The hymn "I Sing the Mighty Power of God" paints a beautiful picture of the Father creating, guiding, and sustaining His creation. As we acknowledge that we ultimately aren't in control, we can give thanks to the One who is:

While all that borrows life from Thee
Is ever in Thy care;
And everywhere that we can be,
Thou, God, art present there.

What does this have to do with first-time experiences? Well, remembering that our Creator has allowed the circumstances in life for our greatest good and His glory is the key. It is not our job to try to control every aspect of what happens to us. We don't have to carry the weight of manipulating our circumstances to make them unfold as we think they should. Our one job is to live in love with Him each day, and what naturally emerges from that will be the greatest outcome possible. So when we step into that new thing, we can step more boldly knowing that it is all happening under the umbrella of His sovereignty. May we always choose to live in His love.

Father, it's such a relief to know that every detail of my life is in Your hands. I need to claim that truth boldly when anxiety shows up to steal my peace and joy. I want to let go and enjoy the journey with You, whatever that looks like today. Thank You for creating and sustaining this magnificent universe and for giving me a chance to experience it all.

AMEN.

THE LORD'S MY SHEPHERD

BE STRONG AND COURAGEOUS.
DO NOT BE AFRAID OR IN DREAD OF THEM,
FOR THE LORD YOUR GOD IS
THE ONE WHO IS GOING WITH YOU.
HE WILL NOT DESERT YOU OR ABANDON YOU.
DEUTERONOMY 31:6 NASB

Many of us have found comfort in Psalm 23 through the years. As soon as we start to hear or read that familiar opening line, "The Lord is my Shepherd," a sense of peace and assurance settles in. It's extra meaningful during times when we're feeling a little insecure and most need to know that we're deeply loved, protected, and cared for in every way. As the psalm takes us on a journey through lush pastures and beside still waters, it also acknowledges the fact that we will encounter "enemies" along the way. And that's to be expected anywhere in life, even in the most ideal environments. As long as we live in this world, there will always be darkness and light. But as we're continually reminded in God's Word, there is nothing to fear, no matter who or what we face. Our loving Father is always willing to provide the very best for us—even in the midst of those who would wish the worst on us.

Of course, if it were up to us, conflict would be something we'd never have to face. Most of us don't set out looking for it. Who needs that kind of negativity, anyway? Who has the energy to manage those tough relationships with people who just seem bent on our downfall? We may believe that if another person has something against us, we can find a way to win them over with the love and grace we've been given in Christ. And sometimes that is what happens! But it's not always the case. Not everyone is open to what we have to offer, and it's not our job to manage that for them. We can knock on the door of their heart, but we can't force our way in. We can only be ourselves, and not everyone will like us or understand who we are. That's just how it works . . . but it still hurts sometimes. That is when we can lean into our loving Father, feel His arms around us, and find comfort in His presence regardless of our circumstances. The hymn "The Lord's My Shepherd" sets those familiar words of Psalm 23 to music:

> *My table Thou hast furnished*
> *In presence of my foes;*
> *My head Thou dost with oil anoint,*
> *And my cup overflows.*

If someone seems to have ill will toward us, we can respond accordingly and be brought down to that level, or we can bless them and move on. Even if we're stuck in an environment with a person who has something against us, we can ask the Lord to help us set healthy boundaries and find a peaceful distance. We can pray for them daily, knowing that prayer may not change the situation or the other person, but it can always change us and our experience. Most importantly, we can walk with God the best way we know how and trust that He will take care of the rest.

Lord God, as much as I wish there was no such thing as conflict,
I know it's just part of living in a broken world. I need Your
help to navigate those difficult connections in my life. May I
always offer grace when I can, set healthy boundaries when
I need to, and remember that You cover me in the spiritual
realm no matter what. Because of Your presence, I know I have
nothing to fear.

AMEN.

BEULAH LAND

*BUT JESUS HIMSELF WOULD OFTEN SLIP AWAY
TO THE WILDERNESS AND PRAY.*
LUKE 5:16 NASB

O h, those naysayers in life—you know the ones. The moment a new dream or idea comes out of your mouth, they seem bent on shooting it down. Hopefully you don't have many negative voices clouding your sky at the moment, but as we've all discovered, they are bound to cross our paths at some point. One of the most critical times to protect ourselves from that kind of influence is when we're finding the courage to follow a God-sized dream. When there's something we feel a strong calling to do and we've confirmed it as best we can with taking prayerful steps in the direction we feel the Spirit is leading, we then need every ounce of support from within and without that we can muster. We know that some of the greatest things we can do for others is loving and accepting them as they are—and that includes the "Negative Nellies" around us. Jesus certainly did that. Even if He had a higher calling for those near Him, He always met them first where they were and loved them unconditionally. *But* He also clearly had boundaries. He knew when He needed to step away from the crowd and recharge. He knew that He couldn't spend every waking moment with every human on the planet, and perhaps that's why there were twelve in His inner circle instead of twelve hundred. We can live with a heart full of love and kindness without allowing ourselves to be continually drained by those who take more than they give. Remember this: we are vessels, and vessels are not used for everything, everywhere, all the time. That means that while we can always be kind to the people in our life, there are times when it is wise to keep our emotional distance from those who are bringing us down. Sure, they have their own reasons for being that way. They may be coming out of a tough past or dealing with a difficult present or even still healing from a crushed dream of their own. We can always offer ourselves to the Lord as an encourager to them, but we can acknowledge that we have needs too. He knows that about us, and He will only call us to pour out what we're able to at the moment. If we listen closely, we'll have peace about those connections. We'll get a sense of both when we need more space and when we can be more available. You may have heard of the old hymn "Beulah Land":

O Beulah Land, sweet Beulah Land,
As on thy highest mount I stand,
I look away across the sea,
Where mansions are prepared for me.

It is all about that strength and hope we have through our eternal connection with Christ. It gives us an unshakable foundation to stand on as we answer His call in our lives regardless of the influence of others around us. As we fix our eyes on the hope of heaven, we will have the courage to let go of anything that blocks our path—even the connections hindering our progress. Remember: it's not about being unkind or unloving; it's about being *His* and trusting that He holds every heart in His hands. He knows who needs what and when. All we need to do is show up each day and be open to anyone and anything He brings into our life.

Lord Jesus, thank You for the example You set. Thank You for reminding us that it's okay to set boundaries, to step away at times, and to follow the voice of the Spirit over any other thing in our lives. Please bless my endeavors and help me to carefully discern who can best support me on the path.

AMEN.

BEULAH LAND

I've reached the land of corn and wine,
And all its riches freely mine;
Here shines undimmed one blissful day,
For all my night has passed away.

O Beulah Land, sweet Beulah Land,
As on thy highest mount I stand,
I look away across the sea,
Where mansions are prepared for me,
And view the shining glory shore,
My Heav'n, my home forevermore!

My Savior comes and walks with me,
And sweet communion here have we;
He gently leads me by His hand,
For this is Heaven's borderland.

A sweet perfume upon the breeze
Is borne from ever-vernal trees;
And flow'rs that never fading grow
Where streams of life forever flow.

The zephyrs seem to float to me,
Sweet sounds of Heaven's melody,
As angels with the white-robed throng
Join in the sweet redemption song.

HOME OF THE SOUL

MY PEOPLE WILL LIVE IN PEACEFUL DWELLING PLACES,
IN SECURE HOMES, IN UNDISTURBED PLACES OF REST.
ISAIAH 32:18 NIV

The word "home" holds meaning for every person. If we grew up in a place where we felt safe, loved, and accepted as a child, it may warm our heart to think of that word today. Some of us moved a lot, making "home" not attached to a certain structure but instead more about the people. Wherever our family was together, that's what we called "home." Hopefully these days we're each able to say that whatever space we inhabit feels like a haven for us in some way. Especially during those times when our days are physically or mentally draining, the rest and refreshment of a welcoming abode is extra wonderful. Surely the sense of warmth and belonging we feel in our own earthly space is a dim reflection of that ultimate homegoing we anticipate—the one that ends in the arms of Jesus. There are many hymns that speak of the joy we will experience in that place where we truly belong. "Home of the Soul" is one of them:

> *Home of the soul, beautiful home,*
> *There we shall rest, never to roam;*
> *Free from all care, happy and bright,*
> *Jesus is there; He is the light!*

We know that souls were designed to find complete fulfillment in the presence of our Maker. There will always be a part of us longing for our true home with Him, because we know we're not quite there yet. But He gave us all we need to get as close as possible while on earth when He gave us Jesus (our Emmanuel, "God with Us"). The more Christ-centered our earthly homes become, the more they reflect the ultimate peace, joy, and fulfillment that we are destined for. And when life feels a little uncertain, home can mean that much more to us. It can be our sanctuary—and just like every other thing in life, our God desires to be present there in every possible way. If we're overwhelmed with clutter . . . if we've ignored things and neglected our space for too long . . . if there's discord among the people under our roof . . . it's going to affect our experience there at home. Yes, we are gloriously imperfect humans living in sometimes-messy spaces, but there are always small, practical steps we can take toward a more harmonious homelife. Sometimes there are very specific reasons for unrest we feel there. It's worth taking some time to look around and consider what weighs on us within those walls. What feels disorganized, out of balance, or just seems to steal our joy when we walk through the doorway? Of course, we can't fix it all at once; things take time (especially relationships!). But we *can* begin to make realistic goals that help bring peace to our space. We can even ask our Maker where to start. Why not? Nothing is too small or insignificant to bring to Him. He knows just what we need and delights in helping us make it happen. He knows that the more present we can be in that place, the more we can enjoy *His* presence. What could be a greater gift than that?

Father, please bless my living space with Your peace, fill it with Your joy, and help me to see anything that prevents me from feeling Your presence there. Thank You for giving us these earthly sanctuaries that reflect our ultimate home with You.

AMEN.

GOD, THAT MADEST EARTH AND HEAVEN

WHEN YOU LIE DOWN, YOU WILL NOT BE AFRAID;
WHEN YOU LIE DOWN, YOUR SLEEP WILL BE SWEET.
PROVERBS 3:24 NIV

There's something so sacred about the nighttime. The gradual hush of our surroundings, the quiet of the house, the moon's rising and stars appearing one by one against an infinite black backdrop. It's a wondrous thing to behold. Even though many of us now live in an around-the-clock culture, no one can deny the rhythm that is revealed by nature, both around and within us, as the days and nights come and go. Our Creator has designed us for both good work and peaceful rest, and one is not really possible without the other. When we "spend" ourselves during the daylight hours, we're more than ready for that pillow when the lights go out. And when we allow ourselves the sleep we need, we are more able to greet the morning with renewed energy. The hymn "God, That Madest Earth and Heaven" speaks of that pattern. It's a prayer honoring God's presence with us around the clock:

> *God, who made the earth and heaven,*
> *Darkness and light:*
> *You the day for work have given,*
> *For rest the night.*

Many of us will *go, go, go* the moment the alarm goes off and shakes us from our dreams. We know just how to jump-start our bodies, and we do what we must to keep them running for as long as we need. But often when nighttime descends, we feel like we just can't shut things down. Whether it's because of our thoughts or our tasks, it can be hard to surrender to sleep—but it's so important that we do. Our bodies can run on fumes for a while, but anyone who has made it to the point of extreme exhaustion will tell you to do whatever you can to avoid experiencing burnout. Ironically, it is often during those seasons when our days are *more* demanding that we allow ourselves *less* sleep. But that's actually when we need all the body and soul reinforcements we can get. One-third of our lives seems like a lot to spend sleeping, but it's a big investment in the two-thirds that we spend awake. God designed our bodies to do some amazing work while we're resting. Our immune system, metabolism, hormones, brain function, and emotional well-being (just to name a few!) are all affected by the amount of sleep we get. During our most stressful times in life, those night hours are especially vital to help us move through the days with more peace and balance.

We've all heard a story about people praying daily for something and God sending an answer that was proverbially right in front of them, but since they were looking for a different miracle, they missed it. As we pray for His help to be the best versions of ourselves that we can be, let's remember that sometimes we forget about tools He has already given us. And one of those tools is rest for our body and soul. If that's something we need more of, we can trust that He will help us make it happen. What can we adjust? What can we let go of? What are some small steps we can take to ensure that our days are filled with more joy and energy because our nights have done the job they're designed to do?

Lord, it's hard to slow down sometimes,
but I know how much I need to! You have created my body
to thrive within that life-giving rhythm of good work
and sweet rest. Please show me what simple steps I can take
in order to live as my best self each day.

AMEN.

SOLDIERS OF CHRIST, ARISE

FOR THOUGH WE LIVE IN THE WORLD,
WE DO NOT WAGE WAR AS THE WORLD DOES.
THE WEAPONS WE FIGHT WITH ARE NOT
THE WEAPONS OF THE WORLD. ON THE CONTRARY,
THEY HAVE DIVINE POWER TO DEMOLISH STRONGHOLDS.
II CORINTHIANS 10:3-4 NIV

Many hymns have been written throughout the years about spiritual warfare. And while it's been defined in many ways, one way to look at a spiritual battle is the leveraging of everything that God promises against everything that opposes God's purposes. The old hymns remind us not to look to our own strength to battle the opposition, but to the One who has given Himself for us, who provides everything we need to live a victorious life. "Soldiers of Christ, Arise" is a wonderful example of that encouragement:

Stand then in His great might,
With all His strength endued,
But take, to arm you for the fight,
The panoply of God.

If you don't use the word *panoply* very often, here's one definition: "a complete set of arms or suit of armor." In Ephesians 6:14-17, Paul tells us to put on the armor of God: the belt of truth, the breastplate of righteousness, shoes of peace, the shield of faith, the helmet of salvation, and the sword of the Spirit. That's a lot to remember in the morning as we walk out of the bedroom and into real life. It's hard enough some days to find clean socks! But here's the point: Our spiritual selves matter infinitely, and they need just as much (or even more!) daily protection as our physical selves. And not only that, but when we are entering new territory in life, it's extra important to be fortified for the journey.

Think of an army from the past (back before all the fancy technology we have these days)—an army that has been camped in one place for a long time. They've learned the lay of the land. They know the vulnerable spots and the safe places. They have a good idea of how the enemy will try to attack, because they've become familiar with it. Now think of what happens when that army has to move to a new area. They don't know where their weak points are yet and aren't sure what route the soldiers from the other side will try to take. So they begin to explore and make a plan. Their preparation will be vital for their survival. Fast forward to today. Say we find ourselves in a new place in life. Whether it's a wonderful transition we've been anticipating or an unexpected change that takes some adjustment, it's still uncharted territory for us. As we allow God to lead us through, there will be great opportunities for growth and goodness. But (as much as we wish it weren't true!) there will also be that opposing spiritual power that will use any tactic to try to bring us down. That's where the armor comes in. It's a vital time to be covered in prayer—both our own and anyone we may ask to lift us up. There's nothing for us to fear or dread in any situation because we know that our Savior stands victorious over it. As we keep our eyes on Him and ask daily to receive all He has for us, He will cover us as He promised and we will find plenty of peace and joy in the journey.

Lord Jesus, You are the One who stands for me, fights for me, and claims victory over the darkness on my behalf.
When I wake each morning, I want to remember that.
I know I need the powerful truth of Your Word, especially in times of change and transition. Help me to hide it in my heart so that I can stand strong on Your promises each day.

AMEN.

COME, LET US SING OF A WONDERFUL LOVE

JESUS SAID, "THE FIRST IN IMPORTANCE IS,
'LISTEN, ISRAEL: THE LORD YOUR GOD IS ONE;
SO LOVE THE LORD GOD WITH ALL YOUR PASSION AND
PRAYER AND INTELLIGENCE AND ENERGY.'
AND HERE IS THE SECOND: 'LOVE OTHERS
AS WELL AS YOU LOVE YOURSELF.' THERE IS
NO OTHER COMMANDMENT THAT RANKS WITH THESE."
MARK 12:29-31 THE MESSAGE

If you've ever watched someone attempt a really big jump from one place to another, you can probably recall that (if they were smart!) they weren't trying to carry anything with them. We all know the science of it: the lighter the load, the kinder gravity will be on the way from point A to point B. Now imagine someone standing there ready to take that leap but insisting on carrying a suitcase in each hand. You'd probably say something like, "Hey, you don't have to do that! If you put those things down, you'll have a much better chance of crossing that chasm there!" It's obvious to you that they simply need to drop the bags, but for whatever reason, they feel obligated to drag them along.

That kind of thing can happen as we're making any kind of shift in life. Whatever that "leap" looks like for us, we would be wise to consider lightening our load as much as possible to prepare for it. One big thing we can put down is the list of expectations we often carry for ourselves. Entering new territory can bring out our insecurities, making us hypervigilant about proving and protecting ourselves— one reason Jesus reminds us to keep things simple ("Don't worry. Don't judge. Don't pretend. Just love."). For some reason, we humans are masters at complicating matters. When we're facing any kind of transition in life, be it a new opportunity, situation, or season, He is merely asking one thing of us: "Follow me." It's the same thing He asks of us every other day of our life. And, as we know, to follow Him is to walk in love—love for God and for those around us. Simple, right? Not *easy*, of course, but *simple* . . . as in a single priority that puts everything else into perspective. The hymn "Come, Let Us Sing of a Wonderful Love" reflects on the sweetness and simplicity of living in that wonderful love of our Savior:

Come to my heart, O Thou wonderful love,
Come and abide, come and abide,
Lifting my life till it rises above
Envy and falsehood and pride.

So . . . love God. Love others. That's it. How is it that we so easily stress ourselves out with lists of additional requirements like, "Make a good impression so you'll be liked by everyone" . . . "Get everything right the first time; don't screw up!" . . . or "Make sure people know how capable you are." These are the kinds of expectations we may not even know we're carrying. We're hard on ourselves because we want to ensure our success. And while it's great to be respected, well-liked, and good at things, we *don't* have to live with that kind of pressure. In the end, we're not running the show anyway. The result is ultimately just not in our hands. That's the wonderful thing about following Jesus: if we focus on His simple call to walk in love, we can trust that everything else will unfold from there.

Lord, what are those expectations I hold over myself that
You see and I don't? What burdens do I carry that
You don't intend for me to bear?
Help me let go of all that weighs me down.
I want to focus on Your simple call to walk in love every day,
in whatever way You lead me.

AMEN.

COME, FOLLOW ME, THE SAVIOR SPAKE

SO FROM NOW ON WE REGARD
NO ONE FROM A WORLDLY POINT OF VIEW.
THOUGH WE ONCE REGARDED CHRIST IN THIS WAY,
WE DO SO NO LONGER. THEREFORE,
IF ANYONE IS IN CHRIST, THE NEW CREATION HAS COME:
THE OLD HAS GONE, THE NEW IS HERE!
II CORINTHIANS 5:16-17 NIV

One way we're called to follow Jesus is by learning to see the world as He does. When we come to know Him, we are offered a new perspective—a new way of seeing everything and everyone. And no matter how long we've been on the journey, we will need our perspective to be renewed from time to time. It's like cleaning a smudged bathroom mirror or wiping a camera lens now and then. How do we do it spiritually? We consider how closely we've been walking with Him, and we lean in all the more. The hymn "Come, Follow Me, the Savior Spake" delivers that simple message we need to hear over and over again:

> Come, follow Me, the Savior spake,
> All in My way abiding;
> Deny yourselves, the world forsake,
> Obey My call and guiding.

During His time on earth, Jesus showed people what it looked like to walk a radically different path than what others in their culture chose to do. A big part of that different way was how He saw and treated people, choosing love over law, grace over judgment, and compassion over criticism. No matter who He encountered, He delivered this powerful message in countless ways: "That is how the world sees you . . . but this is how *I* see you. There's no need to hide anymore. I love you just as you are." We can only imagine what it must have felt like for a person who'd been considered "unclean" or "flawed" to have someone look upon them with such pure acceptance. Or for those who'd been considered unworthy of anyone's attention, to feel the warmth of His smile and the tenderness of His loving gaze. One thing that's clear about Jesus is that He takes no one at face value; He knows how much more is going on beneath the surface of every human being, and He will not settle for a shallow encounter. He takes time to understand people from the inside out, refusing to accept the stereotype or stigma placed upon them. Of course, this was unacceptable to some of the "powers that be" in His time, because everyone knew who was worthy to be honored and who wasn't even worth acknowledging.

While we're playing different roles and dealing with other issues a few thousand years later, we're still human beings who long to be seen and accepted for who we truly are—and there are many among us who continue to be forgotten and misunderstood. One of the greatest gifts we can offer one another is to see through the new eyes He gave us, from a perspective that no longer sets one above the other or judges the proverbial book by its cover. If we want to take our spiritual temperature, we can consider how we're seeing and treating those around us. That will always give us a pretty good idea of how close we're walking with Him.

Lord, I want to see the world more and more the way You do. I want to walk with You, lean into You, and become aware of everything hindering my vision. May I be a vessel for Your love and grace today, offering Your tender gaze to those who need it most.

AMEN.

I WANT TO BE A WORKER

I PRAISE YOU, FOR I AM FEARFULLY AND WONDERFULLY MADE. WONDERFUL ARE YOUR WORKS; MY SOUL KNOWS IT VERY WELL.
PSALM 139:14 ESV

The beloved children's book writer Theodor Seuss Geisel (aka Dr. Seuss) is credited with the saying, "Why fit in when you were born to stand out?" He is known for stories that explore our uniqueness as human beings and the gift of understanding and caring for one another, despite those things that make us different.

Here's a neat thought: could it be (from the outside, looking in) that Christians look all alike? Ask yourself: Does anyone really stand out? After all, we do our best to live our lives by the same truths in God's Word, we gather together regularly in similar spaces, sing the same songs, and may even use some of the same language to explain this indescribable faith journey. With all of these similarities, some might believe that Christians have a "herd mentality" because we belong to a very big group of believers. Sure, we are influenced by those on the journey beside us (hopefully in all the best ways!), but that's only a small part of the story. The truth is that when it comes to living out our faith in our own spheres of influence, we may look very unlike each other. In fact, most of our lives as Christians are lived in those practical spaces at home, school, work, or in the community—wherever we are as individuals, living out what we believe in everyday ways. Those are the places we "stand out" as we live this faith of ours . . . not because we're trying, but because we're living out God's truth in the special ways He has designed for us. It's not going to look the same for any two people. There's so much that goes into how we walk the path—our personality, cultural background, generation, circumstances. Our lives are like a big soup of uniqueness that will never be repeated.

Think of the millions of followers of Jesus and how we each reveal His love to the world in one-of-a-kind ways. We can trust that wherever He leads us to do His good work, He will give us plenty of opportunities to shine for Him. Our job is to relax, be our uniquely created selves, and watch daily for those little opportunities to share His love. The hymn "I Want to Be a Worker" reveals that simple heart's desire we have in common as believers:

> *I want to be a worker for the Lord,*
> *I want to love and trust His Holy Word,*
> *I want to sing and pray,*
> *Be busy every day*
> *In the vineyard of the Lord.*

What sets us apart from our brothers and sisters in Christ? A lot of things! What do we share in common? We're coworkers, working for Him every day, each in our own way. And no matter how often that "vineyard" of life changes, we just keep doing our thing however He calls us to. When we look around and see others who share our faith, doing *their* thing in their way, we can encourage them to keep being themselves for Him too. We can celebrate both what we have in common and what's different about us, knowing that both are gifts God has given to the world to know Him through all of us.

Lord, thank You for my spiritual family. I'm so grateful that
no matter where I go, I can find fellow workers for Your
kingdom. Give me the confidence to be the unique self
You created, trusting that Your love will shine through me
in whatever way You intend today.

AMEN.

O GOD, OUR HELP
IN AGES PAST

REMEMBER YOUR HISTORY,
YOUR LONG AND RICH HISTORY.
ISAIAH 46:9 THE MESSAGE

If you grew up with close ties to your extended family, you probably know that wonderful feeling of walking through a front door without knocking. Seeing familiar faces on the other side or open arms offering warm hugs—maybe soothing voices saying your name in a way that made you feel as if you were cherished more than any other human being on the planet. You may remember the wonderful smells of your grandmother's kitchen, the delicate treasures that sat on a favorite aunt's bookshelf, or the sound of giggles coming from all the cousins piled into the bed in the guest room. And even if your loved ones lived halfway across the country, you may have piled into the car and traveled many miles just to spend time with those who meant the most to you.

Being surrounded by our loved ones and savoring all those wonderfully familiar sights, sounds, and smells of our growing-up years helped to create that picture of childhood we carry in our heart today. There's a feeling of warmth, familiarity, and security when we recall time spent in the presence of those who've loved us unconditionally all our lives. They remind us who we are and where we came from. They give us the gift of knowing that no matter how lost we may feel in this great big world or how unsure we are of our purpose, there is someone who has known us from the beginning and will be there to support us as long as they are on this earth. We all know that life can get crazy sometimes. Unexpected things happen, big changes show up unannounced, and we find ourselves reeling a little (or a lot) and needing to feel grounded again. Those occurrences may be good times to turn to the loved ones we share a deep connection with . . . whether that means knocking on a familiar door or calling someone who is miles away. Talking with a parent, grandparent, or someone else who has been on this life journey longer than we have can help renew our faith during times of uncertainty. Even if we were not raised in a Christian family, there are likely a few of our loved ones (or even longtime friends) who share our beliefs. Hearing their stories of walking through challenging times can always lift us up and give us courage. The hymn "O God, Our Help in Ages Past" offers us the assurance that comes with remembering who He has always been for us:

O God, our help in ages past,
Our hope for years to come,
Our shelter from the stormy blast,
And our eternal home.

Just as we experience that warmth and comfort from the lifelong connections we share with our earthly family, we can find a wonderful sense of security in our eternal connection with our Father. All our loving relationships in this life reflect His heart for us in some way, and we can trust that He will always be here among us to calm our heart during those times we need it most.

Lord, the lifelong love of family is a priceless gift
and a beautiful reminder of Your eternal love.
Help me recall those wonderful connections You have provided,
especially when I encounter times of uncertainty.
Just as You have sustained every generation of believers,
I trust that You will see me through.

AMEN.

BREATHE ON ME, BREATH OF GOD

THE SPIRIT OF GOD HAS MADE ME, AND THE BREATH OF THE ALMIGHTY GIVES ME LIFE.
JOB 33:4 NKJV

Think about your breath for a moment—the sound of it, the mystery of it, the way it has been with you every minute of your life. That inhale of yours was the first thing you did when you were born, and exhaling will be the last thing you do as you leave this earth for your heavenly home. In between those two moments will be many, many breaths taken. (To give you an idea, by the time you're eighty years old, it'll be close to 700 million!) Sometimes those breaths will be deep and restorative, and other times they'll be shallow and anxious. That "inward/outward" flow definitely reflects what is going on inside of you . . . and not just physically, either. Throughout Scripture, we read about the idea of breath representing God's Spirit. From the creation of Adam, when He "breathed into his nostrils the breath of life" (Genesis 2:7 NKJV), to Jesus filling the disciples as "He breathed on them, and said to them, 'Receive the Holy Spirit'" (John 20:22 NKJV). There is something so powerful about this process that sustains our physical and spiritual life. The hymn "Breathe on Me, Breath of God" is a short and sweet invitation for God's Spirit to fill us and make us His own:

> *Breathe on me, breath of God,*
> *Fill me with life anew,*
> *That I may love the way You love,*
> *And do what You would do.*

We often hear people say "Take a deep breath" when we're feeling nervous about something, or we breathe "a sigh of relief" when it's over. That's because our bodies and minds are so intricately woven together by our Creator that one will always affect the other. If we are anxious in mind, we will feel it everywhere. And if we can remember to slow down and return to our breath in those times, we'll feel more at peace and less stressed.

We can always take a spiritual breath too. God has given us ways not only to refresh our physical and mental selves, but He has also provided "spiritual oxygen" in the form of His Word and His presence in creation. When we find ourselves in a situation or a season that takes a toll, this can make a huge difference. We can find those promises in His Word that allow us to relax and let go a bit. You know the ones that speak to your heart—the ones that make your spirit breathe a sigh of relief because they reflect the peace, joy, and freedom you possess in Christ. Keep those promises close, especially during stressful times.

Another powerful breath of fresh air He has provided for our spirit is the natural world around us. You know what elements speak to your soul. Seek out what brings you a sense of calm and assurance, be it stargazing, gardening, or laying in a hammock while watching the tree branches sway above you. Wherever you most experience His presence, find time there for those spiritual breaths. The longer we practice this, the more we'll be able to carry His peace through any situation—mind, body, and spirit—as we breathe in His truth and exhale His love toward all we meet.

Lord, the mysteries of Your creation are endless,
and I marvel at the detail with which You made each of us.
Every breath we take is a gift from You,
and I want all of mine to be for Your glory.
Remind me often to breathe deeply in every way,
resting in Your presence and giving thanks
for this life You have given me.

AMEN.

NOT I, BUT CHRIST

JESUS LOOKED AT HIM AND LOVED HIM.
MARK 10:21 NIV

If we could somehow interview the people who encountered Jesus during His time on earth, it might surprise us to hear the things they remembered about Him. Of course, they'd speak of the big miracles, the long-awaited healings, and the large crowds that gathered just to see Him pass by. But it's very likely that we would hear about "smaller" things too, details that seem more insignificant compared to some of those epic events that leap off the pages of history. Perhaps people would recall His warm smile and kind eyes or that moment He took to kneel next to a person who'd been discarded by society, speaking their name as if they were the most precious soul on earth. We might hear about the way He listened intently to others or touched their hand in a gesture of comfort and assurance. All very simple actions, to be sure, but they were powerful enough to ripple throughout history because of the divine love they carried within them.

Now think about our world today. Consider the changes we've faced on a global level. Some folks feel confused and frustrated; others are looking for a "new normal"; and still others are seeking opportunities to help big changes for the better. That may be where our work as Christ followers is most needed today—bringing His light to people who are searching more than ever. But we don't have to make some epic attempt to impact the world all at once. Just as Jesus changed lives by the simple gift of His presence, we can too. This is surely one of the most powerful ways to be the hands and feet of Christ in the world today. That's the beautiful message of the hymn "Not I, but Christ:"

Not I, but Christ, be honored, loved, exalted;

Not I, but Christ, be seen, be known, be heard;

Not I, but Christ, in every look and action,

Not I, but Christ, in every thought and word.

While the challenges and issues of our day are different than in Jesus's time, human beings are still the same: the same needs, the same inner struggles, and the same desire to be truly seen, loved, and understood. Simply offering our presence to others in uncertain times can be a priceless gift, and it doesn't take much to do that in our day-to-day lives. Some of us grew up watching a television show called *Mr. Rogers' Neighborhood*. It was hosted by Fred Rogers, a puppeteer and pastor with a deep love for children. One of the things people remember most about Mr. Rogers is his willingness to slow down and be present with each person he came into contact with. Some described his presence as a "sanctuary" because he made them feel safe and surrounded by love. He made a huge impact on his audience and generations to follow not because he was the most outspoken or impressive TV personality, but because he took the time to be fully present with people, just as Jesus did. He allowed his kind words and simple, loving actions to flow out into the world, trusting that the biggest difference was made one person at a time.

Jesus, slow me down and make me aware of the simple needs of the people around me today. May I offer Your presence to those who feel fearful, discouraged, or insignificant. I want to share Your love in some small way with everyone I meet.

AMEN.

NOT I, BUT CHRIST

Not I, but Christ, be honored, loved, exalted;
Not I, but Christ, be seen, be known, be heard;
Not I, but Christ, in every look and action,
Not I, but Christ, in every thought and word.

Not I, but Christ, to gently soothe in sorrow;
Not I, but Christ, to wipe the falling tear;
Not I, but Christ, to lift the weary burden!
Not I, but Christ, to hush away all fear.

Not I, but Christ, in lowly, silent labor;
Not I, but Christ, in humble, earnest toil;
Christ, only Christ! no show, no ostentation!
Christ, none but Christ, the gath'rer of the spoil.

Christ, only Christ, ere long will fill my vision;
Glory excelling, soon, full soon, I'll see—
Christ, only Christ, my every wish fulfilling—
Christ, only Christ, my All in all to be.
Amen.

Dear Friend,

This book was prayerfully crafted with you, the reader, in mind. Every word, every sentence, every page was thoughtfully written, designed, and packaged to encourage you—right where you are this very moment. At DaySpring, our vision is to see every person experience the life-changing message of God's love. So, as we worked through rough drafts, design changes, edits, and details, we prayed for you to deeply experience His unfailing love, indescribable peace, and pure joy. It is our sincere hope that through these Truth-filled pages your heart will be blessed, knowing that God cares about you—your desires and disappointments, your challenges and dreams.

He knows. He cares. He loves you unconditionally.

BLESSINGS!

THE DAYSPRING BOOK TEAM

Additional copies of this book and
other DaySpring titles can be purchased
at fine retailers everywhere.
Order online at <u>dayspring.com</u>
or
by phone at 1-877-751-4347